DISCARD

ADOLF HITLER

Scott Ingram

San Diego • Detroit • New York • San Francisco • Cleveland
New Haven, Conn. • Waterville, Maine • London • Munich

For more information, contact
The Gale Group, Inc.
27500 Drake Rd.
Farmington Hills, MI 48331-3535
Or you can visit our Internet site at http://www.gale.com

Photo Credits: Cover, pages 8, 33, 76, 103 © CORBIS; pages 5, 21, 36, 47, 50, 59, 63 © Hulton-Deutsch Collection/CORBIS; pages 11, 31, 71, 72, 89, 92, 100 © historypictures.com; pages 11 © Bettmann/ CORBIS; page 14 © Gianni Dagli Orti/CORBIS; page 20 © Archivo Iconografico, S.A./CORBIS; page 23 © Christel Gerstenberg/CORBIS; page 27 © Underwood & Underwood/CORBIS; pages 45, 57, 67, 69, 70, 85, 86, 91, 93, 98, 101 © Blackbirch Press archives; page 53 © Austrian Archives/CORBIS; page 95 © Paul Almasy/CORBIS

LIBRARY OF CONGRESS CATALOGING-IN-PUBLICATION DATA

Ingram, Scott.
Adolf Hitler / by Scott Ingram.
p. cm. — (History's greatest villains)
Summary: Examines the birth, family, early years, and political career of Adolf Hitler, discussing his hatred of Jews, involvement in the Nazi Party, role in World War II and the Holocaust, and death.
Includes bibliographical references and index.
ISBN 1-56711-625-6 (alk. paper)
1. Hitler, Adolf, 1889-1945—Juvenile literature. 2. Heads of state—Germany—Biography—Juvenile literature. 3. National socialism—Juvenile literature. 4. Germany—History—1933-1945—Juvenile literature. [1. Hitler, Adolf, 1889-1945. 2. Heads of state. 3. National socialism. 4. Germany—History—1933-1945.] I. Title. II. Series.
DD247.H5 I57 2003
943.086'092—dc21 2002006145

Printed in United States
10 9 8 7 6 5 4 3 2 1

Contents

Introduction: "Rise in Bloody Vengeance" 4

Chapter 1 Childhood in Austria 9

Chapter 2 From Austria to Germany 19

Chapter 3 On the Western Front 29

Chapter 4 After the Defeat 37

Chapter 5 Rise to Power 56

Chapter 6 Nazi Power Spreads 68

Chapter 7 War and the Holocaust 88

Chronology 104

Glossary 106

Source Notes 108

For Further Reading 110

Websites 110

Index 111

Introduction: "Rise in Bloody Vengeance"

By the evening of November 9, 1938, the leaders of Germany's National Socialist Party had spent a long day in joyous celebration. The Nazis, as they were known, had marched, feasted, and congratulated one another on the anniversary of their party's first attempt to take power in 1923. That event, known as the Beer Hall Putsch, had failed. The man who organized the putsch, Adolf Hitler, was tried and sentenced to prison. In November 1938, 15 years later, Hitler was no longer a prisoner. He was the führer—the supreme leader—of Germany.

As Hitler and his supporters concluded the daylong festivities, word passed to the führer that a Nazi diplomat in Paris had died of gunshot wounds. The young man who shot the official was a Jewish teenager named Herschel Grynszpan. He had shot the Nazi to avenge the deportation of his family to Poland.

As soon as he heard about the diplomat's death, Hitler pulled aside his spokesman, Joseph Goebbels. The führer angrily told Goebbels that it was time to attack Jews throughout Germany. Hitler left the celebration and did not make a speech to the crowd.

The führer's suggestion was all the encouragement Goebbels needed. The death of a low-level diplomat presented a perfect opportunity for him to unleash his intense hatred of Jewish people. When he rose to speak, he announced the news of the diplomat's death to the large crowd of Nazi officials. It was now time, said Goebbels, to "rise in bloody vengeance against the Jews."

When Goebbels finished his speech, the people in attendance jumped into action. Dozens of phone calls from the celebration hall set a chain of events in motion that came to be known as *Kristallnacht*—the Night of Broken Glass.

In the early hours of November 10, mobs of Nazi Party members, street thugs, and other Germans burst into Jewish homes, businesses, and synagogues across Germany and Austria. Homes were ransacked; stores and businesses were destroyed. Synagogues were set on fire and Jewish holy books thrown into the flames. Jewish men, women, and children were beaten and taunted. As the violence took place, local firefighters and police officers watched and did nothing.

Nazis destroyed more than 7,000 Jewish-owned businesses and burned more than 300 synagogues.

Synagogues, such as this one in Berlin, were set on fire during the Night of Broken Glass.

Ninety-one people were killed, and thousands were beaten and tortured. More than 30,000 Jews were arrested and sent to concentration camps. Several days later, the Nazis blamed the Jews themselves for the destruction and fined the Jewish people of Germany and Austria one billion marks.

Over the days that followed *Kristallnacht*, nations around the world condemned the anti-Jewish riots in Nazi Germany, but Hitler, Goebbels, and other Nazi leaders were more interested in the German response. Across the country, voices were silent. Germans either agreed with what the Nazis had done, or they were too frightened to speak out. Either way, the Nazis knew, their rule was unchallenged.

CIGARREN

Chapter 1

CHILDHOOD IN AUSTRIA

Three-fourths of the world's population, more than 1.7 billion people in 61 countries, were in some way involved in World War II (1939–1945). More than 110 million soldiers fought battles in Asia, Europe, and Africa. About 20 million of these members of the military died. Huge numbers of civilians also died in World War II. In fact, civilian deaths greatly outnumbered the military deaths.

Among those who died in the war in Europe were 20 million Russians. More than 7 millions Germans died, and 6 million Poles

Opposite: By the early 1930s, millions of young Germans looked up to Adolf Hitler as a hero.

were also killed. The toll also extended to religious groups, ethnic minorities, and other groups. More than 6 million Jews were murdered by the Nazis, as well as 5 million Roma (sometimes called gypsies), Jehovah's Witnesses, mentally and physically disabled people, and homosexuals. The persecution and attempted mass extermination of Jews and other minorities is known as the Holocaust.

Although he had willing assistance from allies and fellow Nazis, one man was largely responsible for the conditions that cost the lives of tens of millions of people. That man was Adolf Hitler.

Decades after his death, it is hard to imagine how this homeless Austrian came to have so much power and was able to win the devotion of the people of Germany, even though it was not his native land. Adolf Hitler, one of history's villains, swore that under his rule, the world "would have no other god but Germany," and he came very close to achieving his goal.

Early Years

Adolf Hitler was born on April 20, 1889, in Braunau am Inn, a small village in Austria, near the border of the German state of Bavaria. His father, Alois, was 52 years old, had been twice widowed, and had two other children when Adolf was born. The baby's mother, Klara Pölzl, was 29 years old, and had given birth to three children who died in infancy before Adolf's birth. She favored Adolf, even after she later gave birth to another son and a daughter.

Above: Alois Hitler was a stern disciplinarian. Below: Klara Pölzl was a loving mother.

Alois Hitler had grown up in a difficult environment. He was born Alois Schicklgruber to 41-year-old Maria Schicklgruber, and he never knew his father. His mother died when Alois was 10, and he was sent to live with an uncle, whose last name was Hiedler. Alois moved to Vienna, Austria, where he applied for a civil service job and became a customs official.

Shicklgruber rose through the civil service ranks and became a supervisor at age 39. At that time, his elderly uncle—who was proud of his nephew's success—offered to put Schicklgruber in his will if he changed his last name to Hiedler to carry on the family name. Schicklgruber agreed, but the clerk who filled out the records made a mistake and spelled the last name "Hitler."

In 1885, Alois Hitler married Klara Pölzl, who was Hiedler's granddaughter. This meant that Alois Hitler actually married his niece, which required special approval from the Catholic Church. The couple settled in Branau am Inn with Hitler's two children from a previous marriage—Alois Jr., and Angela. In 1894, five years after Adolf, Edmund Hitler was born, and two years later, Paula was born.

School Years

Alois Hitler was able to provide quite well for his family with his government salary. In 1895, Adolf's first year in school, his father retired on a pension. Because his father had succeeded professionally as a demanding supervisor, he also set high standards for his children. He handed out severe punishment if the children did not meet those standards.

Adolf was a lazy student who preferred to draw rather than study. His father would not tolerate poor grades and often beat his children—and possibly his wife. Alois Hitler's beatings were so frequent that his oldest son, Alois Jr., eventually left home and never returned. From that point on, Adolf's father turned all of his fury on Adolf, and the boy returned his father's anger and hatred.

At age 11, Adolf's life changed dramatically. His younger brother, Edmund, died of measles at age six. It was Adolf's first experience with death, and he was moody and withdrawn for months.

That same year, his primary school years ended. Adolf's father wanted him to attend a school that would prepare him for a university and then a civil service career. Adolf, whose main interests were drawing and architecture, wanted to attend a technical school to develop those skills. Eventually, Alois Hitler gave in and sent Adolf to a nearby technical school in the large city of Linz, Austria.

Old and New Empires

The location of Linz, near the German border, drew many people from Germany to live and work there. Relations between the two nations were peaceful, and the city was a mix of German and Austrian cultures. Even so, at the end of the nineteenth century, when Adolf went to Linz, the two nations were different in several ways.

At that time, Austria was part of what was known as the Austro-Hungarian Empire. It had been ruled for centuries by kings from a family known as the Hapsburgs. The empire was populated by several different national

Otto von Bismarck

Otto von Bismarck (1815–1898) was the man primarily responsible for the creation of the German empire. For centuries, the country known today as Germany was a loose confederation of kingdoms ruled by nobility. In the 1860s, Bismarck served as minister of the German kingdom of Prussia. It was then that he chose his mission in life: to create a unified German empire. "My highest ambition is to make the Germans a nation," he said.

Otto von Bismarck united German states into an empire.

In 1866, after a series of wars in Europe, Bismarck formed an alliance between Prussia and 17 other German states. In 1871, the German empire—called a reich—was established. William I of Prussia was declared the kaiser, or emperor. Bismarck was appointed the reich chancellor, a position similar to that of prime minister.

Once political unity was achieved, Bismarck set out to establish a relationship between Germans and their new empire. Bismarck believed individuals had no reason to distrust the state, so the only requirement of a good German was complete obedience to the kaiser and the legislature, which was known as the Reichstag. There was no reason to question any decision the state made and no need for democratic principles such as separation of powers or checks and balances.

Bismarck's rigid ideas caused conflict with several organizations. One was the Catholic Church. Another was the Socialist political party that represented workers' interests against the wealthy men who were elected to the Reichstag. In both cases, Bismarck passed laws that effectively took rights away from the church and political leaders who opposed him.

By the time Bismarck left office in 1890, Germany was one of the most powerful military and political powers in the world. Although he had created a unified state, Bismarck had also discouraged political dissent. In 1899, a German historian wrote, "In our nation . . . the individual man, even the best among us, never rises above doing his duty in the ranks."

groups, including Hungarians, Germans, Poles, and Slavs, all of whom who spoke different languages and had different cultures. The empire, once one of the most powerful in Europe, was in decline as its people began to assert their national identities and agitate for independence.

Germany, on the other hand, was a powerful young empire formed in the 1870s by a statesman named Otto von Bismarck. Although the German empire—called a reich—comprised former kingdoms, such as Prussia, Bavaria, Silesia, and others, all of its subjects spoke similar versions of the German language. They also shared a common culture that included myths from as far back as the days when the Germanic tribes conquered Rome in the third century A.D. As an impressionable teenager from a small village, Hitler learned and absorbed many aspects of this culture. He soon began to believe his ancestors had been German.

A Failed Student

While Hitler was away at school in the city of Linz, Alois Hitler died in 1903, at the age of 65. Even without him, the family was financially sound, supported by his yearly pension. In addition, the government paid each child a monthly sum until he or she left home.

After his father's death, Adolf failed several courses and was told that he would have to pass special exams to continue in the technical school. A teacher noted that 15-year-old Adolf "lacked self-discipline, being notoriously cantankerous, willful, arrogant, and bad-tempered. In freehand sketching, his style was fluent and he did well in scientific subjects. But his enthusiasm for hard work evaporated all too quickly."

Adolf was able to pass his tests and continue with his education. To give him a more stable life closer to school, his mother and younger sister moved to Linz, and the three rented an apartment in the city. Eventually, because of his poor study habits, Adolf had to take a special exam to graduate from the technical school. Unwilling to put in the time needed to study, he convinced his protective mother that he was not well enough to continue with school. With no diploma and no job, Adolf usually slept late and took daily strolls through the Linz city parks.

Adolf was a pale, skinny youth, who sometimes carried a black cane as he walked through town. He became friends with a young man named August Kubizek, who hoped to become a professional musician. Kubizek described his friend as "exceedingly violent and high-strung." Hitler, said Kubizek, could not stand to be corrected by anyone and often flew into rages if someone pointed out a mistake.

A Turning Point

By 1907, Hitler had made up his mind to pursue a career as an artist. To do so, he planned to attend one of Europe's finest art schools, which was located in Vienna, the capital of Austria. In October 1907, 18-year-old Hitler went to Vienna to take the two-day entrance examination for the famed Academy of Fine Arts.

In one of the biggest disappointments of his life, Hitler was rejected. According to the academy's report on his work, his drawings were "unsatisfactory." Examiners said he especially lacked the ability to draw human portraits.

Hitler returned to Linz to receive even more shattering news. His mother was dying of breast cancer. Hitler had known that his mother was ill before he left for Vienna. Klara Hitler had been diagnosed with cancer the previous January, but after an operation that removed a breast, her health seemed to improve. When Hitler had gone to Vienna, he believed that his mother was on her way to recovery.

When he returned, Hitler was too dejected about the results of his test to tell his mother of his failure. When he saw how her health had worsened, he consulted her doctor, Eduard Bloch. The doctor told him that only the most drastic cure had any chance of success. The treatment required Hitler to apply a compress of iodine directly on the cancerous ulcers on his mother's chest. Hitler stayed by mother's side day and night applying the compresses.

Despite Hitler's devoted care, Klara died on December 21, 1907. It was the greatest loss of Hitler's life. Bloch said that he had never seen anyone as grief-stricken as Hitler was over the death of his mother.

Klara Hitler was buried in the same cemetery where Edmund had been buried. Hitler's younger sister, Paula, went to live with their half sister Angela. Hitler decided to return to Vienna and try once again to pursue a career in art.

CHAPTER 2

FROM AUSTRIA TO GERMANY

In the winter of 1908, Hitler and his friend Kubizek found an apartment together in Vienna. At that time, Vienna had a population of about 2 million people from the numerous Eastern European nations in the empire. The city also had a population of about 180,000 Jews, many of whom dressed in traditional religious clothing that made them stand out from most other Viennese.

For a number of months, Hitler was able to live on the pension from his father much as he had in Linz. He read, slept late, walked in parks, and made sketches. Occasionally, Kubizek and Hitler would

Vienna, Austria, was a cultural center for much of the 1800s.

attend the opera. One of the most popular opera composers of the day was Richard Wagner. He was a strong German nationalist, which appealed to the young Hitler. Wagner was also an anti-Semite—a person prejudiced against Jews.

Rejection and Homelessness

In early 1909, Kubizek returned to Vienna after an absence of several months for military training to find that Hitler had moved out. For the next two years, Hitler drifted aimlessly around Vienna. He read constantly, and usually concentrated on works of philosophy, history, and mythology. He spent evenings in clubs, where he argued about politics or philosophy. He gained a reputation as a strange young man who became hysterically angry with anyone who contradicted him.

Richard Wagner was one of the most renowned composers of his day.

Hitler soon had to sleep on park benches and under bridges. He ate at soup kitchens and asked passersby for handouts. Eventually, he moved into a homeless shelter called the Männerheim. Each resident had a tiny room in which to sleep, and there were several large common rooms where men gathered to read, talk, or work on hobbies. By the winter of 1910, Hitler was 21 and could no longer receive his father's pension. He was forced to seek work as a day laborer. He shoveled snow or carried baggage for passengers at the Vienna train station to earn a few coins.

Although he had failed in his pursuit of an art career, Hitler continued to draw and paint. To develop his abilities, he drew precise sketches of well-known buildings in Vienna. He decided to sketch the buildings on postcards and sell them. Hitler soon began to paint watercolor landscape scenes of Vienna that were larger than postcards. He was able to sell these as well.

Even at this low point in his life, Hitler continued to read and debate political issues. He often gave impromptu speeches to other residents of the shelter, and became furious if anyone interrupted him or disagreed with his ideas. A fellow resident of the shelter

ANTI~SEMITISM

Anti-Semitism, the hatred of Jewish people, has existed for thousands of years. Much of this prejudice originally arose because of religious differences between Jews and Christians. In the years immediately after the death of Jesus Christ, the Christian faith spread from the Middle East into Europe. At about the same time, Jewish people were expelled from their homeland, the modern country of Israel, after they revolted against the Roman empire. This expulsion was known as the Diaspora, or dispersion.

Some Jews migrated to other Middle Eastern countries or along the northern coast of Africa. Many others migrated to northern and eastern European countries, where they encountered prejudice because of their religion and culture. Acts of violence were frequently committed against Jews throughout the Middle Ages, a time when a number of myths and stereotypes about Jewish people began. In some areas of Europe, people believed that Jews used the blood of Christian children to make the bread they ate during a religious holiday. Jews were also blamed for the spread of the bubonic plague, a disease carried by fleas, that killed one-fourth of Europe's population in the Middle Ages.

Stereotypes that depicted Jews as dishonest also arose at that time. Laws in many regions forbade Jews to own land. In many cases, the only way Jews could earn a living was to become merchants or shopkeepers. No matter where they attempted to settle, Jews were often forced out of a region very suddenly. Thus, many Jews began to convert any local money they earned into gold, which had value anywhere. Eventually, some Jewish people turned to one of the few ways possible to earn a living—they loaned gold for a profit. It was not unusual, then, for a European community to have a Jewish moneylender. Because the Christian religion had laws that said it was wrong to loan money for profit, the practice increased resentment and suspicion among people who were already prejudiced against Jews for religious reasons.

Anti-Semitism existed throughout Europe for more than 1,000 years, and Germany was one region in which it was especially strong. The founder of the Protestant branch of Christianity, a German named Martin Luther, was one of the most vehemently anti-Semitic religious leaders in history. When Jews refused to convert to his new version of Christianity in the 1500s, he called them the "anti-Christ" and said they were "worse than devils." Luther said Jews were parasites who should be expelled from Germany. He also encouraged Christian Germans to burn synagogues and Jewish holy books.

Although hatred of Jews existed for centuries, the term anti-Semitism was first used in the mid-1800s by a German named William Marr. Marr founded a group called the League for Anti-Semitism, which put forth the belief that all Jews were physically and morally inferior to the group called Aryans. According to Marr and his followers, Aryans were Germanic and Nordic people.

During this time, mass murders of Jews began to take place in areas of Poland and Russia. These mass killings were known to Jews as pogroms, a Hebrew word that meant "devastation." The pogroms coincided with the spread of anti-Semitism in Germany, and with Hitler's early years in Austria.

A fifteenth-century woodcut shows Jews being burned alive.

recalled that "when Hitler became excited he couldn't restrain himself. He screamed and fidgeted with his hands." During evenings at the shelter, men gathered to discuss literature, music, and art. Hitler took part in order to sharpen his debating skills. Sometimes these discussions became shouting matches as Hitler defended Austria's majority political party, the anti-Semitic Christian Socialists, or attacked those who held liberal political views.

Few men at the shelter believed that Hitler was any more anti-Semitic than many Austrians at that time. Some of Hitler's favorite artists and musicians were Jewish. He often praised Jewish charities that had helped him survive. He even had two Jewish friends at the shelter. One of them, Josef Neumann, helped Hitler sell some of his artwork.

Throughout 1910, Hitler read political pamphlets. He also read German history and mythology books from the library. The works he read helped Hitler gradually form his own political philosophy, a system of beliefs based on racism, nationalism, and anti-Semitism.

At this time, many middle- and upper-class Austrians in Vienna were anti-Semitic. The mayor of Vienna, a member of the Christian Socialist Party, was openly anti-Semitic—and extremely popular with the people of

Vienna. Hitler admired the mayor's speeches, especially the way he used the most exaggerated stereotypes to persuade his audiences to support anti-Semitism.

Move to Munich

In the spring of 1913, at age 24, Hitler left Vienna for Munich, the capital of Bavaria in Germany. Munich was smaller than Vienna, with a population of about 600,000. Hitler left Austria to avoid service in the Austrian army. He also hoped to enter Munich's Academy of Art, which was less demanding than the academy in Vienna.

Hitler never did become a student there. Instead, he sold paintings door-to-door. As he had done in Vienna, Hitler borrowed books from the library and spent his evenings reading. He often went to beer halls where he joined political discussions. Hitler did not drink, but he found the beer halls a good place to debate.

In January 1914, the Austrian authorities located Hitler, and he was ordered to report to Linz to serve in the army. Failure to report would result in a prison sentence. Hitler did report to take the army's physical exam, after which he was rejected for military service because of his weak physical condition. Hitler then returned to Munich.

World War I Erupts

Less than a month after Hitler's rejection from the Austrian army, the assassination of the heir to the Austrian throne set the stage for the greatest war the world had yet known. On June 28, 1914, Archduke Franz Ferdinand and his wife were assassinated by a man named Gavrilo Princip in Sarajevo, Bosnia. Princip was a native of Serbia, a country that had long been under the control of the Austro-Hungarian Empire, but had a growing nationalist movement.

The assassination set a number of events into motion that rapidly grew violent because of the tangled alliances of European nations. In July, Austria-Hungary declared war on Serbia and attacked Belgrade, the Serbian capital. Russia then entered the war to defend its ally Serbia. That action in turn drew Germany, an ally of Austria-Hungary, into the conflict. At that time, France was an ally of Russia. Germany, which was located between France and Russia, declared war on France. That brought England to join France in a declaration of war against Germany and its allies. By mid-August 1914, World War I had begun.

Most Germans approved of the decision of Kaiser Wilhelm, Germany's ruler, to enter the war. In Munich, Hitler was among the enthusiastic crowd that cheered

The First Modern War

At the outbreak of World War I in August 1914, people on both sides were confident that the war would end quickly. Four years later, the clash of traditional nineteenth-century concepts of warfare and the twentieth-century modernization of weapons had shocked the world.

Life in the trenches was brutal and filthy.

World War I was fought mainly in trenches that ran from Switzerland across France to the North Sea. Both opposing armies dug miles of ditches from which they fired at the enemy. The armies were separated by open ground called "no-man's-land." Neither side in the war advanced more than three miles once the troops were dug into trenches. Troops that attempted to advance ran into barbed wire and minefields. Waves of soldiers were cut down by a deadly new weapon, the machine gun.

Men on the front lines lived in mud and filth. Diseases such as "trench mouth" and "trench fever" afflicted men who were crowded together month after month in muck. Even the removal of dead bodies became difficult during intense artillery shelling that went on for weeks.

In addition to machine guns, armies on both sides used a new weapon that took a terrible toll—poison gas. Shells packed with chlorine, ammonia, or other poisonous gases blistered soldiers' skin, blinded them, and burned their lungs.

The number of troops killed in the war reached numbers far beyond those of any earlier conflict. Even before the trenches were established, each side had lost more than 500,000 men. The French lost more than 1.5 million men in 1915. In the five-month Battle of the Somme in 1916, the Germans lost more than 600,000. On one day in 1917, 20,000 British soldiers were killed. The United States did not enter the war until April 1917, but by the time the war ended in November 1918, more than 50,000 Americans had died in battle. In all, more than 10 million soldiers died in World War I and more than 10 million civilians died from fighting, disease, and starvation.

A British soldier's recollections summed up the gruesome conflict: "We pushed [the bodies] into the sides of the trenches but bits of them kept getting uncovered and sticking out, like people in a badly made bed. Hands were the worst; they would escape from the sand, pointing, begging—even waving! There was one which we all shook when we passed, saying, 'Good morning'.... The bottom of the trench was springy like a mattress because of all the bodies underneath."

the announcement of the war. Although he was Austrian by birth, Hitler eagerly supported Germany and took part in parades to show support for the kaiser.

For an aimless loner such as Hitler, the war was a chance to become involved in what he saw as a noble cause: the glory of the German empire. He wrote that World War I "began the greatest and most unforgettable time of my earthly existence. Compared to the events of this gigantic struggle, everything past receded to shallow nothingness."

Although he had been rejected for service in Austria, Hitler sent a letter to the Bavarian government in which he asked permission to join the German army. He was accepted, and in August 1914, Hitler became a member of the First Company of the 16th Bavarian Reserve Infantry. On October 21, the troops were loaded onto trains and transported to the front lines.

CHAPTER 3

ON THE WESTERN FRONT

Hitler's first battle was against British and Belgian forces near Ypres, Belgium. The inexperienced soldiers in his unit were ordered to advance through dense fog to relieve another unit that had established a trench position. As the Germans inched forward, artillery shells exploded in the woods ahead and cut trees into splinters. "We crawl on our stomachs to the edge of the forest," Hitler wrote to a friend in Munich. "Above us are howls and hisses . . . shells explode at the edge of the forest and hurl clouds of stones, earth and sand into the air . . . and choke everything in a yellow-green, terribly stinking steam."

The Battle of Ypres continued for four days. Of the 3,000 men in Hitler's regiment, about 2,500 were killed or wounded. Hitler performed admirably during the battle as a messenger. Because telephone contact between front lines and command posts was often destroyed and messages could be intercepted, runners were needed to carry urgent messages.

Unlike most soldiers, Hitler did not complain about army food or the filthy conditions of the trenches. Instead, he talked about art and history, and his discussions often turned into lectures. In his two years at the war front, Hitler never asked for leave. Other soldiers thought he was likable but rather odd. They also believed he was incredibly lucky—several times he left areas just moments before shells hit. Hitler claimed that he heard voices that told him to move before shells landed:

> *I was eating my dinner in a trench with several comrades. Suddenly a voice seemed to be saying to me, 'Get up and go over there.' It was so clear and insistent that . . . I rose . . . and walked twenty yards along the trench. . . . Hardly had I done so when a . . . shell . . . burst over the group [with] which I had been sitting, and every member of it was killed.*

During the summer of 1916, Hitler, now a lance corporal, moved south with his regiment to take part in the Battle of the Somme, a river north of Paris. The battle began as an attempt by British and French forces to break through German lines. The first day of the battle was one of the bloodiest days in military history. More than 65,000 soldiers were killed or wounded.

Hitler, seated last on the left, poses with his fellow soldiers.

On October 7, 1916, Hitler was asleep in a narrow tunnel that connected two trenches. A shell exploded near the entrance of the tunnel and wounded him in the thigh. Although he asked to remain at the front, he was taken to a field hospital. It was his first time away from the war front in two years.

After his release from the hospital, Hitler returned to Munich. Much to his disgust, Hitler found that the people's support for the German war effort had faded over the last two years, and there was an active antiwar movement in the city. He believed that the antiwar sentiment was part of a Jewish conspiracy to cause the collapse of Germany. Hitler eventually returned to his old regiment in 1917.

Revolution and Unrest

At the same time that Hitler returned to the western war front, millions of Russian peasants and workers revolted against their ruler, Czar Nicholas II. The Russian Revolution overturned centuries of absolute rule by monarchs. The leaders of the revolution followed the political ideology of Karl Marx, who wrote a book titled *The Communist Manifesto*. This work described a philosophy called Marxism or Communism, which took power and property away from the wealthy few and redistributed it to the workers.

The Russian Revolution left the nation in turmoil and made it less of a threat to the Germans. Hitler was pleased by the Russians' gradual withdrawal from the war, because he felt that all of the German military could now be repositioned in France. Nevertheless, Hitler despised Marxism because it supported a worldwide revolution of workers and opposed the idea of national borders and cultures. In addition, Karl Marx was a Jew, as were many of the first Communists in Russia, which added fuel to Hitler's anti-Semitic beliefs.

The Russian Revolution began in St. Petersburg, Russia, in 1917.

A month later, in April 1917, the war took another turn when the United States entered it on the side of the French and British. The arrival of almost 500,000 fresh troops gave the Allied powers—Germany's enemies—a tremendous boost.

Problems on the front lines, as well as unrest among workers who supported the Russian Revolution, strengthened the antiwar movement in Germany. In January 1918, workers across the country went on strike to demand peace. In Berlin, 400,000 workers left their shops. The military forced them back to work within a week, but the country was clearly on the brink of revolt.

As the war—and the defeats—continued, many German soldiers lost their enthusiasm. Soldiers refused to take orders, and many attacked their officers when they were threatened with court-martial. Thousands simply left their weapons in the trenches and walked away from the battle lines.

When he learned of the extent of rebellion in Germany and observed the low morale of his fellow soldiers, Hitler blamed Communists and Jews. He himself carried out his duties to the end. In August 1918, Hitler received the Iron Cross, First Class, one of Germany's highest war medals. This honor was rarely awarded to infantrymen, but Hitler's devotion to duty had been widely noted by his commanders. Hitler also received four other medals for his military service.

Although Hitler performed well in the army, he was never promoted beyond the rank of corporal. His commanders felt that he lacked leadership ability because of his explosive temper.

The war ended for Hitler on October 14, 1918, when he was temporarily blinded in a mustard gas attack and was forced to return to Munich. The fighting on the western front continued until an armistice was signed on November 11, 1918.

On June 28, 1919, the Treaty of Versailles was signed, which formally ended World War I. The Allied nations of France, England, and the United States signed the treaty as did the Central Powers of Germany, Bulgaria, and Turkey. Austria-Hungary had been broken into the separate nations of Austria, Hungary, and Czechoslovakia after the earlier armistice. Thus, the

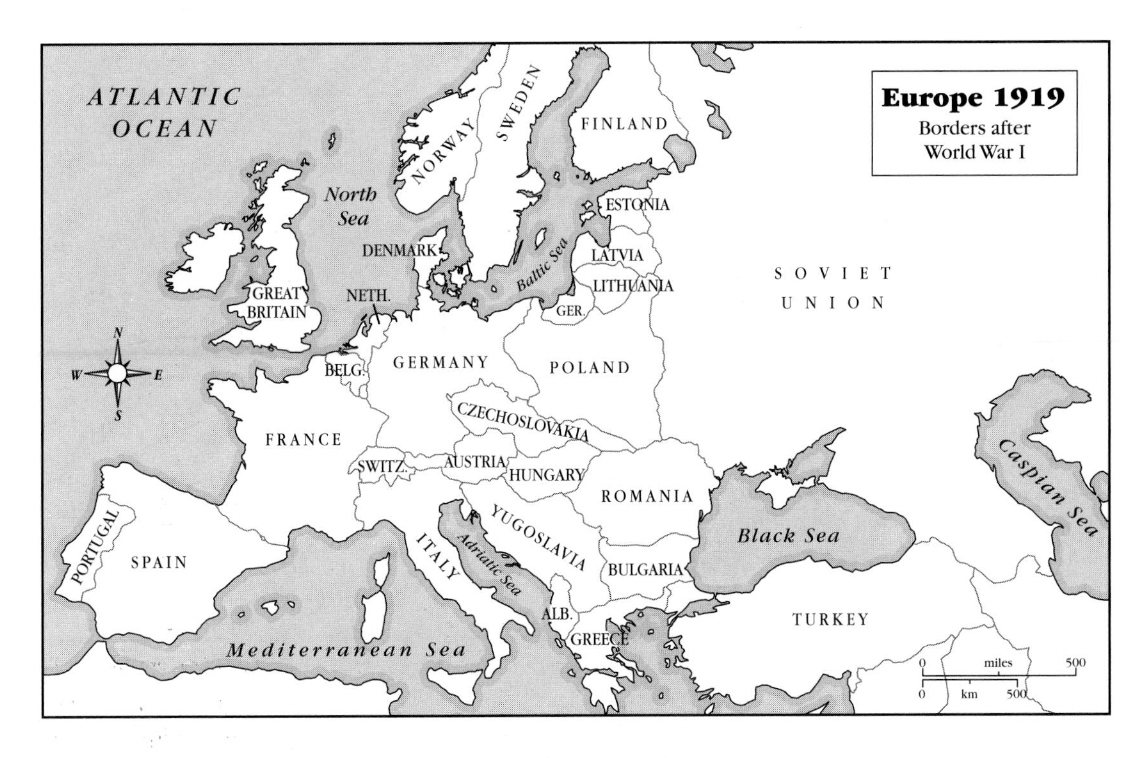

empire did not shoulder any blame for the war damages. For the most part, the treaty placed the blame for the war on Germany.

The Allies forced the German government to ratify the treaty, which left the struggling nation with a huge war debt that it had to pay to the victorious nations. The treaty also limited the German army to 100,000 volunteer soldiers and forbade the Germans to manufacture certain weapons. The armistice and treaty led German generals, as well as veterans like Hitler, to believe that the army had not truly been defeated on the battlefield. They felt that politicians, Communists, and Jews had betrayed them with their antiwar agitation.

At the end of World War I, Berlin was a city of homeless, jobless refugees.

To add to the dismay of the military veterans, in 1919, Germany adopted a constitution unlike any that had ever existed in the country. Political power was placed in the hands of the people, who voted for a German president. Minority parties were allowed representation in the legislature, called the Reichstag. A chancellor, who was the leader of the Reichstag, was elected by a majority vote.

At the time the constitution was adopted, Germany was extremely unstable. Left-wing Marxist groups clashed with right-wing nationalistic groups. In 1919, mercenaries and war veterans in Berlin and Munich murdered scores of Communists, Socialists, and innocent bystanders.

By 1919, Germany was a totally different nation from the way it had been in 1914. The kaiser had been forced from his throne. The Second Reich, founded by Bismarck in 1871, was gone. In its place was a battered nation that was weak in the eyes of the world and humiliated in the eyes of men like Hitler.

Chapter 4

After the Defeat

In the summer of 1919, Hitler was stationed in Munich. The German president, Friedrich Ebert, feared that the civil war caused by the Russian Revolution would spread to his weakened nation. He ordered that Marxists not be permitted to join the volunteer army so that they could not take it over. To keep Marxists out, a secret military group was formed to spy on workers' groups. With his patriotic zeal, Hitler was a natural choice to become an informer, or undercover agent.

Before he attempted to infiltrate Marxist groups, Hitler was ordered to attend classes at the University of Munich for instruction on political philosophy. He later described his experience: "One of the participants . . . began to defend [the Jews] . . . . This aroused me to an answer. The overwhelming majority of the students present took my standpoint. The result was that a few days later I was sent into a Munich regiment as a so-called educational officer."

Hitler's views about Jews impressed the leader of the class, and Hitler soon became a lecturer who warned newly returned German prisoners of war about Communism and pacifism. The soldiers also became a captive audience for his speeches against Jews. These soldiers were eager to have someone to blame for their recent imprisonment, and Hitler provided them with a scapegoat.

In September 1919, Hitler was assigned to investigate a small political group called the German Workers' Party in Munich. The word Workers in the name had aroused the military's interest because it suggested that the party might support Communism. The meeting drew only around 25 people. Hitler was about to leave the meeting when one of the men there suggested that Bavaria should break away from Germany and form a new nation with Austria.

For Hitler, an extreme German nationalist, that was inconceivable. He stood up and spoke angrily against the speaker for 15 minutes. The people in the room were spellbound. When Hitler finished, Anton Drexler, one of the founders of the party, gave him a pamphlet called *My Political Awakening* and invited him to the next meeting. Hitler read the pamphlet and realized that the German Workers' Party actually supported a nationalistic, pro-military, anti-Semitic platform of beliefs.

Hitler soon became a member of the organization. He immediately got to work to try to increase the party's membership. He drew up invitations that members passed out to their friends. A few more people showed up at the next meeting. Then an advertisement was placed in an anti-Semitic newspaper in Munich. The party also moved its meetings to a large beer cellar. On October 16, 1919, about 100 people showed up for the meeting.

Hitler, the second speaker of the evening, displayed an intensity unlike anything the audience had seen before. He later described the scene: "I spoke for thirty minutes, and what before I had simply felt within me, without in any way knowing it, was now proved by reality: I could speak!"

Soon Hitler left the army and became the featured speaker at every meeting of the German Workers' Party. He used the meetings to attack the Treaty of Versailles. He spoke out against the Jews, who he claimed had ruined Germany. More and more people began to come to the meetings—before long, more than 300 people came to each meeting to listen to Hitler.

A New Name and Symbol

In 1920, Hitler became the supervisor of propaganda for the party. In that position, he distributed pamphlets and posters that expressed the party's views. In his desire to increase membership, he also encouraged men he had known in the army to join. Many of these men were disillusioned veterans who missed the adventure of war.

At that time, Marxist groups also increased their membership. Hitler feared that the Communists might become powerful enough to take over the German government. In February 1920, Hitler organized the first large meeting of the party. Other members of the committee felt that it was too soon for a young party such as theirs to hold a large meeting. They also feared that the event might draw Marxists to disrupt it. Hitler explained that such disruption could actually be good propaganda. It would focus attention on the German Workers' Party's anti-Marxist, nationalist beliefs. "It makes no difference whether they [people] laugh at us or revile us, whether they represent us as clowns or criminals; the main thing is that they mention us, that they concern themselves with us again and again," Hitler said.

When Hitler entered a large meeting hall in Munich on February 24, about 2,000 people waited to hear him. Shortly after he began to speak, fights broke out between Communists and members of the German Workers' Party. Hitler continued to speak, and eventually his listeners calmed down. In his speech, he outlined the 25 points that the party claimed would return Germany to greatness. These points included the union of all Germans in a new reich. The party also demanded the return of lands the German people had given up to the Allies after the war. Citizenship in the new reich was based on race. Jews were considered aliens and would not be allowed to hold public office. A strong central government was considered a key element.

As Hitler read each of the points, he asked the crowd for its approval. They applauded and shouted in favor of each point. As the meeting concluded, Hitler believed that the party's first large meeting had been a tremendous success. His only dissatisfaction was with the party's name and its lack of a symbol.

Hitler felt that the party's name, German Workers' Party, was not nationalistic enough. He changed the name to the National Socialist German Workers' Party

(*Nationalsozialistische Deutsche Arbeiterpartei*, or NSDAP), which was often shortened to the Nazi party. By 1920, party membership stood at about 2,000 people.

In the summer of 1920, Hitler developed a symbol for the party. It was the swastika, a twisted cross that Hitler had first seen at a monastery in Austria when he was a child. In ancient times, the shape had been a symbol of blessings and good luck in many cultures. Hitler claimed that the shape had first been used by the "master race," people of Germanic descent whom he believed were superior to all other people. He also claimed that the swastika had been "eternally anti-Semitic," which made it the ideal symbol for the Nazis. He had the heavy black shape placed on flags in a white circle, which represented racial superiority. The circle sat on a red background to represent the blood that would be spilled to achieve the goals of the party.

Five Critical Years

Hitler's powerful speeches—especially his denunciations of the Treaty of Versailles and Jews—soon brought the Nazis to the attention of many Germans in Munich. In February 1921, Hitler spoke in front of a crowd of 6,000 people. Before the event, he had party members toss leaflets to advertise the meeting.

Hitler's next objective was to spread the Nazi movement beyond Munich. In the summer of 1921, he visited nationalist groups in Berlin to find out if it might be possible to join forces. While he was gone, the Nazi Party undermined his leadership. The party's executive committee, of which Hitler was a member, feared that Hitler had become too much like a dictator within the organization. To counter this, they formed an agreement with a Socialist group from a town near Munich.

When Hitler learned what had happened, he resigned from the party. This caught the executive committee by surprise. They knew that Hitler's resignation would mean the end of the Nazi Party. Hitler said that he would rejoin if he were made chairman and given complete control. Some committee members refused to bend to his wishes. A party pamphlet titled "Adolf Hitler: Is He a Traitor?" argued against him and the brutal veterans, such as Hermann Göring, whom he had brought in to gain control of the party. Despite this opposition, the executive committee gave in to Hitler's demands. At a meeting on July 29, 1921, Hitler was introduced as the führer, or leader, of the Nazi Party. It was the first time this title was used to refer to Hitler.

Events related to the Treaty of Versailles soon brought the views of Hitler and the Nazis to the public's attention. In 1921, France and England demanded that Germany pay $33 billion for war damages. The demand made the poor economic conditions in Germany even worse. Inflation caused the value of money to decrease. When the debt to be paid was announced, four German marks were equal to one U.S. dollar. Suddenly the rate became 75 marks to a dollar. By 1922, the value of German money had fallen to 400 marks to a dollar. In desperation, the German government asked the Allies to postpone the payments. When France would not agree, Germany was unable to pay the debt. In response, the French army occupied an industrial part of Germany known as the Ruhr. At that point, the German economy began to decline rapidly. By July 1923, the exchange rate was 160,000 marks to a dollar. By November 1923, it took 4 billion marks to equal one dollar—the mark was basically worthless. Workers still received salaries, but it cost billions of marks to buy a bag of groceries. Anti-government food riots broke out across Germany.

By late 1923, membership in the Nazi Party had reached about 55,000. Hitler believed that as support for the government faded, he might be able to stage a revolt in Munich and take control of the state of Bavaria. He developed a plot to kidnap the leaders of the state government and force them to accept him as the führer of Bavaria. He then planned to use the German army stationed in Bavaria to topple the democratic government in Berlin.

To accomplish the first part of his plan, Hitler formed a core of tough men into a uniformed paramilitary unit. At first, this group was used for crowd control at large meetings. Soon, however, the *Sturmabteilung*, called the SA for short, became Hitler's private army. The storm troopers, as they came to be known, were placed under the leadership of Hermann Göring, Hitler's old acquaintance from the army.

Early members of the Nazi Party marched in Munich in 1922.

Hitler and the other Nazi leaders put their plan into effect on November 8, 1923, when a large number of Munich businessmen met at a beer hall. The guests of honor were the Bavarian leaders Hitler planned to kidnap. Göring led a group of storm troopers that surrounded the beer hall. Then Hitler and other storm troopers burst into the hall. Hitler fired a pistol at the ceiling and announced that the Bavarian government had been dismissed and a Nazi government was in control.

Hitler brought the three members of the Bavarian government to a back room. These officials included a state commissioner, the head of the state police, and the commander of the German army in Bavaria. Hitler offered these men posts in the new government. The three officials refused to respond to the offer, and Hitler threatened them with his gun.

In the midst of the excitement, Hitler received word that the SA had met resistance as it tried to take over several army barracks. Hitler left the beer hall and went directly to the barracks. His absence allowed the three Bavarian officials to escape. Unable to force the soldiers at the barracks to surrender, Hitler returned to discover that the officials and the crowd were gone.

The next morning, the state commissioner issued a statement that condemned Hitler and ordered the Nazi Party to be dismantled and the SA disbanded. German army forces marched into Munich and surrounded the SA troops.

Rather than surrender, Hitler decided to parade into Munich. He believed that his public support was so

Hitler (left) was one of several Nazis who organized the Beer Hall Putsch.

strong that the people would not allow the Munich police and army units to fire at him.

On the cold morning of November 9, about 3,000 Nazis formed a column led by Hitler and Göring. Hitler's personal bodyguards marched to his left. In the middle were experienced storm troopers. Following them was a collection of men in business suits and work clothes, and veterans in uniforms with swastika armbands.

As the Nazis approached the War Ministry building, they encountered a police blockade. Someone—most likely one of the Nazis—fired. A gun battle began.

Within minutes, 14 Nazis and 4 police officers were dead. Göring was wounded. Hitler had linked arms with a man who was shot, and as the man fell, he dislocated Hitler's shoulder. Hitler's bodyguard jumped on top of Hitler to shield him and was shot several times. Hitler crawled along the sidewalk and jumped into a car, while the rest of the Nazis ran for their lives. Hitler fled to the home of a friend. On November 11, he was arrested and put on trial for treason for his action in the revolt that became known as the Beer Hall Putsch.

The judges in the trial were chosen by a Bavarian official who was sympathetic to the Nazis. At his trial, Hitler was allowed to speak as long as he wanted to and cross-examine witnesses. After 24 days, Hitler gave a closing statement, part of which showed his contempt for the trial and his belief that the Nazi Party had widespread support.

The court found Hitler guilty, and he was sentenced to five years in prison, the minimum sentence. The judges, who had become sympathetic to the Nazis during the trial, also made him eligible for parole, which meant that he would probably be released early.

On April 1, 1924, Hitler was taken to Landsberg, Bavaria. There, he was confined in a military prison, where he was given a comfortable private cell with a view of the mountains. During his time in prison, Hitler wrote a book called *Mein Kampf* (My Struggle). The book was partly an autobiography, but it also explained his political and racial philosophies.

According to Hitler, Aryans—Germanic people with fair skin, blond hair, and blue eyes—were superior to all other groups of people. Though he considered himself part of this "master race," Hitler himself had dark hair and dark eyes. Hitler claimed that the Aryans had developed the art, science, and technology that the world enjoyed. Hitler stated that other peoples benefited when they were conquered by Aryans because they learned from a superior culture. In *Mein Kampf*, Hitler called those people he considered racially inferior the *Untermenschen*—subhumans. These included dark-skinned people and those of Slavic origin, such as Czechs, Poles, and Russians. The *Untermenschen* also included Jews.

It was the Aryans' destiny to rule the world, said Hitler, and it was the Jews who did not allow them to assume their rightful position. "The mightiest counterpart to the Aryan is represented by the Jew," Hitler stated. He claimed that the Jews had formed an international conspiracy to control world finances. He said they controlled the press, had invented Marxism, and had

Protocols of the Elders of Zion

Hitler's belief in a Jewish conspiracy was not his alone. During the years before and after World War I, anti-Semitism flourished in Europe and the United States. Contributing to this prejudice was a book called the *Protocols of the Elders of Zion*. The book was supposed to be the notes of an 1897 meeting of Jewish leaders in Switzerland at which they discussed "protocols," or procedures, for world domination. In truth, the book was written sometime between 1895 and 1899 by an agent of the Russian secret police named Pytor Rachovsky, who was known to have forged documents for the police.

The first publication of the *Protocols* was in Russian. It was published in Europe to be used as proof that Jews were behind the Revolution. A Russian named Boris Brasol brought the work to the United States around 1920, where it formed the basis of an anti-Semitic movement founded by car manufacturer Henry Ford. Ford published excerpts of the work in his anti-Semitic collection of essays, *The International Jew*.

Although the book was known to be a fake as early as 1921, the *Protocols* became a key part of Nazi propaganda. *The International Jew* and the *Protocols* became the two main texts for Nazi anti-Semitism. In *Mein Kampf*, Hitler described the importance of the book to his program of anti-Semitism: "Anyone who examines the historical development of the last hundred years from the standpoint of this book will at once understand... the Jewish menace."

A German copy of the Protocols of the Elders of Zion.

spread disharmony throughout the world. Whenever Hitler discussed Jews in his book, he referred to them as dirty, crafty, and clever liars. According to Hitler, the ultimate battle for world domination would be fought between Aryans and Jews.

In *Mein Kampf*, Hitler stated that Aryans, the "master race," had the right to take land from other peoples. This land, which he called lebensraum (living space), included territory east of Germany in Poland and Russia, where food could be cultivated and the German population could expand. To get this living space, Hitler wrote, Aryans had the right to remove, eliminate, or enslave other peoples.

Hitler was released from prison in December 1924, after he had served nine months. His time there had brought him to the conclusion that he could use the process of election to win control of the German government. He planned to organize the Nazi Party so that it resembled a government, and when he was elected to head the German government, he would put Nazis into key positions.

He faced just one problem. During his time in prison, the Bavarian government had banned the Nazi Party. Early in 1925, Hitler met with the prime minister of Bavaria and convinced him to permit the Nazi Party to reorganize. Hitler promised that the Nazis would follow democratic policies.

On February 27, Hitler addressed a large meeting of Nazis and claimed his position as absolute ruler of the party. In his speech, he denounced Jews and made threats against the democratic republic. As a result, the Bavarian government did not allow Hitler to speak in public for two years. Hitler decided to use this time away from the public eye to restructure the Nazi Party.

Expansion and Organization

Under Hitler's new plan, the Nazis divided Germany into 34 districts, each with a leader. Each district was divided into smaller segments, and the smaller units were broken into *Ortsgruppen*, or local groups. In this way, the Nazi Party was able to bring its message to every corner of Germany. The leaders could determine where they had the most followers and where they needed more recruitment.

The Nazis next organized the Hitler *Jugend*, or Hitler Youth, for boys who were 15 to 18 years of age. Younger boys were allowed to join the *Deutsches Jungvolk*. Girls could enter the *Bund deutscher Mädel*.

Hitler also reorganized the military arm of the Nazi Party, the SA. In *Mein Kampf*, he stated that the storm troopers were "an instrument for the conduct and reinforcement of the movement's struggle for the philosophy of life." He had SA members wear brown shirts, boots, swastika armbands, badges, and caps. Within the SA, Hitler formed another group to serve as his personal elite force. He called this group the *Schutzstaffel*, the staff guard or SS, and its members wore black uniforms.

Paul von Hindenburg was a hero to many German veterans of World War I.

The main problem the Nazis faced when they tried to persuade the German people to accept Nazism was that Germany's economy had begun to recover. As the country's economy improved, fewer people were attracted to the extreme Nazi philosophy. Hitler was not worried, since he did not think the improvement would last and he believed Germans would continue to join his party. Another obstacle was the new president of Germany, Paul von Hindenburg, who had been a hero of World War I. Middle-of-the-road political parties as well as conservative groups supported him. Despite these problems, Hitler continued to prepare his followers to take advantage of any political or economic tensions that arose.

By May 1926, Hitler had removed any competition for leadership of the Nazi Party, and the party was united behind his philosophy. During this time, Nazi official Joseph Goebbels became the person closest to Hitler. Goebbels was an educated man with a graduate degree in literature. A highly skilled speechwriter and a master of propaganda campaigns, he shared Hitler's intense hatred of Jews.

Goebbels was sent to Berlin, the capital of Germany, to became a Nazi district leader in the city, which had not been a stronghold of Nazi support. In the elections of May 1927, the Nazis did not receive many votes nationally. Through his political skill and his clever use of propaganda, however, Goebbels was elected to a seat in the Reichstag.

The Great Depression

In October 1929, the economic disaster that Hitler had hoped for took place. The world financial industry, centered in the stock market on Wall Street in New York City, collapsed. The crash seriously damaged the economies of nations around the world. Banks failed. Companies closed down almost overnight. Millions of workers lost their jobs. The stock market collapse began the era known as the Great Depression.

Before the Great Depression, the Nazi Party had about 100,000 members in a nation with a population of more than 60 million people. As small as the party was, Hitler believed he could expand his power through elections. He was aided by the fact that there were no dominant parties in Germany at that time. By 1930, Hitler had gained the financial support of important German business leaders and upper-class people who believed the Nazis would restore the nation's financial health.

In March 1930, Heinrich Brüning, a member of the Catholic Center Party, became chancellor, the chief minister of Germany. Brüning tried to develop a plan to pull Germany out of the Great Depression, but other political parties with different views refused to cooperate with him. Brüning then asked Hindenburg to use Article 48 of the German constitution, which gave the chancellor the power to act as a dictator in time of emergencies. Those who opposed Brüning argued against the use of Article 48, and he withdrew his demand. Instead, Brüning asked Hindenburg to hold a new election, in the hopes that his party would gain enough seats to push through his program. The elections were set for September 14, 1930. This gave Hitler a great opportunity to put Nazi Party members into the Reichstag.

Chapter 5

Rise to Power

In 1930, the Nazis conducted a massive election campaign across Germany. Hitler traveled and spoke around the country. He shook hands with voters, signed autographs, and kissed babies. In his speeches, Hitler promised work for the unemployed, prosperity for businesses, peace, and, most of all, a return to the past glory of Germany.

On election day, the Nazis received more than 6 million votes, about 18 percent of the total. They won 107 seats in the Reichstag, which made the Nazis the second largest political party in Germany.

To celebrate their victory at the polls, Nazi storm troopers, dressed in civilian clothing, smashed the windows of Jewish shops and restaurants.

On October 13, 1930, brown-shirted Nazi Party members marched into the Reichstag to take their seats. Over the following year, German business leaders donated huge amounts of money to the Nazis, whom they expected would soon take over the leadership of the nation.

Early in 1932, Hitler was asked to meet with Brüning, who wanted Hitler's support for another seven-year term for Hindenburg. Hitler refused. Instead, in February, Hitler decided to run for president against the 84-year-old Hindenburg with the slogan, "Freedom and Bread."

Nazi storm troopers with guard dogs were a frightening sight to many Germans.

In the presidential election, held in March 1932, Hitler received more than 11 million votes, about 30 percent of the total. Hindenburg received almost 19 million votes, or 49 percent. Because no candidate received a majority, a runoff election was scheduled for

April 10. For a month, Hitler campaigned tirelessly around the country. Hindenburg campaigned very little.

On April 10, Hitler received almost 37 percent of the vote. Hindenburg won 53 percent. Hitler had received 2 million more votes than the last time. Hindenburg had gained fewer than one million. Hitler had lost, but the Nazis had displayed their organizational strength and growing popularity.

Even though the party was popular, by 1932, many Germans had serious concerns about the SA and SS troops. The storm troopers had grown into a private force several times the size of the German army. In April, Brüning used Article 48 of the constitution to ban the Nazi troopers. Hitler temporarily agreed to the ban because he needed the support of the German army and businessmen. Both groups were disturbed by the Nazi forces.

Storm Troopers in the Streets

Hitler's agreement to keep his forces under control did not last long. On May 8, 1932, Kurt von Schleicher, a powerful army officer whose dream was to lead Germany, had a secret meeting with Hitler. He wanted Nazi support to form a conservative nationalist government. In return, Schleicher promised that once he took over the government, he would dissolve the Reichstag and call for new elections. Then he would lift the ban on the SA and SS. Hitler agreed to the deal.

Kurt von Schleicher was one of the most powerful generals in the German army.

Brüning became Schleicher's main target. The chancellor had begun to help restore the German economy, but he had also angered several political groups when he used Article 48 to pass his programs. As he became increasingly unpopular, Brüning made a disastrous mistake. He proposed that the huge estates of wealthy people who had gone bankrupt be broken up and given to poor farmers. To many Germans, his proposal sounded like a Communist plan. In May 1932, Hindenburg asked Brüning to resign, and Brüning agreed.

Schleicher now exerted control over the government from behind the scenes. With the votes of the Nazis and other nationalistic parties assured, he chose Franz von Papen as the chancellor. Papen assembled a cabinet of wealthy aristocrats and businessmen. On June 3, the Reichstag was dissolved and a new election was planned for the end of July.

Hitler held up his end of the agreement and supported Papen. As a result, on June 16, the ban on the SA and SS was lifted. Immediately, the storm troopers took to the streets, where they beat people and destroyed property. Gun battles between Nazis and Communists broke out in several cities. In order to stop the violence, Papen used Article 48 to impose martial law and named himself Reich Commissioner, a position that gave him dictatorial powers.

With the government on shaky footing, Hitler sensed that an election victory might be in his grasp. He continued to speak before audiences of 100,000 people or more. On July 31, a new election gave the Nazis 37 percent of the total vote. With 230 seats in the Reichstag, the Nazi Party was now the strongest political party in Germany.

On August 6, Hitler demanded that Schleicher gather political support to put him in position to win the chancellorship of Germany. He also wanted an act passed in the Reichstag that would give him complete control of the government.

Hindenburg refused to cave in to Schleicher's demands that he nominate Hitler as chancellor, a move that would assure his election. Hitler flew into a rage and threatened to turn the SA loose in Berlin. He quickly reconsidered, however, and faded briefly from the public eye while he considered his next move.

On September 12, Papen, unable to form a consensus in the government, dissolved the Reichstag and called for yet another election. Many Nazis were tired of the frequent campaigns, and their effort was not as enthusiastic as it had been in previous elections. As a result, the Nazis lost 34 seats in the Reichstag.

The Nazi loss, however, did not mean that Papen gained any support. On November 17, he resigned because the Reichstag did not support him. Hitler quickly met with Hindenburg and asked to be nominated for the vacant chancellor's office. Again Hindenburg turned him down, and Hitler decided to remain out of the public eye for a while.

With the government unable to act and food riots in the streets, Hindenburg met with Papen and Schleicher to decide on a course of action. Papen suggested that he return as chancellor, but this time, he wanted to permanently invoke Article 48, dissolve the Reichstag, and rule as a dictator with the support of the army. In other words, Papen said, he would bring back the old German empire. Schleicher dismissed the idea. He claimed that he was the only person with enough power to lead the government and handle the Nazis. After the three men had a loud argument, Hindenburg named Schleicher the chancellor of Germany on December 2, 1932.

Schleicher's first step was to meet with Gregor Strasser, a Nazi who opposed Hitler's dictatorial rule, and to offer him the vice-chancellorship in return for Nazi support. When Hitler found out about the offer to Strasser, he refused to give Nazi support to Schleicher's government.

As political events became more chaotic, wealthy industrialists pushed to have Hitler take power. Papen, who still hoped to become a dictator, wanted to end Schleicher's role in the government. On January 4, 1933, Hitler met with Papen. The two men agreed to work together to make Hitler the chancellor, with Papen as vice-chancellor.

In early 1933, Hitler, Papen, Hindenburg's son, Oskar, and Göring held a secret meeting. Hitler convinced Oskar von Hindenburg to support him. Papen also pledged loyalty to Hitler. On January 28, Schleicher resigned under pressure. On January 30, President Hindenburg gave his support to Hitler as chancellor. It was about noon when Hitler was sworn into office. He was driven down the street, cheered by thousands of Germans. Among those who cheered for Hitler was Eva Braun, a young photographer's assistant from Munich, whom Hitler had met in 1929. The two became companions for the rest of their lives.

On the evening of January 30, 1933, thousands of SA and SS members stood in front of the chancellor's residence. Each man held a burning torch that flickered on the red and white Nazi banners. Men, women, and children waited to see the new chancellor. People listened to accounts of the event on the radio. Finally, Hitler appeared before the adoring crowd. "It is almost like a dream—a fairytale," Joseph Goebbels wrote in his diary. "The new Reich has been born." Because Bismarck's empire had been called the Second Reich, the new reign of Hitler and the Nazis quickly became known as the Third Reich.

Hitler treated Hindenburg respectfully in public.

At the news of Hitler's rise to power, former General Erich von Ludendorff, who had supported Hitler until Hitler demanded absolute power in the Nazi Party, sent Hindenburg a telegram: "I prophesy to you this evil man will plunge our Reich into the abyss and will inflict immeasurable woe on our nation. Future generations will curse you in your grave for this action."

Consolidating Control

On his first day in office, Hitler convinced Hindenburg to dissolve the Reichstag and call for new elections for March 5, 1933. To gain military support, Hitler attended a dinner with the German general military staff. He promised that Germany would rearm and then conquer Austria, Poland, and other lands to the east. Hitler also assured the staff that the SA storm troopers would not replace the army.

On February 22, on Hitler's orders, Göring established a police force of 50,000 men—most of them SA and SS veterans—as a unit separate from the regular German police. This secret police force became known as the Gestapo. On February 24, the Gestapo destroyed the headquarters of the Communist Party in Berlin.

Göring then developed a plan to burn the Reichstag building and blame the Communists. Although the fire was never actually linked directly to any Nazi, on February 27, the Reichstag burned to the ground. The next day, Hitler asked for emergency powers to counter the Communist threat. Immediately, the Nazis began to round up Communists, middle-of-the road Social Democrats, and liberals, who were all herded onto trucks and taken to SA barracks. They were tortured, and fifty-one people died.

Nazi newspapers, under propaganda minister Goebbels's direction, printed false stories about a Communist conspiracy. The articles claimed that Communists and Jews wanted to take over Germany, and only Hitler and the Nazis could stop them. The same claims were made in broadcasts from radio stations across the country.

On March 5, Germany's last free election during Hitler's lifetime was held. The Nazis received only 44 percent of the vote, which was not a majority. Since the Nazi Party organization was already in place in the country, the Nazis simply took over all levels of government by force. State and local government officials were threatened by SA and SS men. They were thrown out of office and replaced by Nazis.

Thousands of people who were considered political enemies of Germany were arrested. The Nazis used abandoned factories and deserted army barracks as prisons. These prisons were placed under the control of the SA and SS.

On March 15, 1933, Hitler held a cabinet meeting to discuss the passage of what was called the Enabling Act. This law, used only during times of war and national crisis, would turn over all the processes of government to the chancellor, Hitler. It allowed him to make laws, set up a budget, and approve treaties with other nations, without the approval of the Reichstag.

On March 21, under pressure from Hitler, Hindenburg signed laws that favored the Nazis. One law pardoned all Nazis held in prison. Another allowed the police to arrest anyone who criticized the government or the Nazi Party. A third law established courts without juries, known as military tribunals, to try people who were arrested for political crimes.

On March 23, the members of the Reichstag met to vote on the "Act for the Removal of Distress from People and Reich." This was Hitler's Enabling Act, which would make him the dictator of Germany. Storm troopers stood in the aisles as the legislature convened. Before the vote, Hitler promised to use the power of the Enabling Act wisely to help Germany economically and in its relations with other nations.

Otto Wels, leader of the Social Democrats, opposed Hitler. "No enabling act can give you power to destroy ideas which are eternal and indestructible," he said.

Hitler, angered at the opposition, stood up. "You are no longer needed!" he yelled. "The star of Germany will rise and yours will sink! Your death knell has sounded!"

The vote was 441 for the act and 84 against. Hitler—with the help of the Reichstag, which had

Hitler drew enthusiastic crowds when he spoke in public.

voted itself out of existence—had effectively ended democracy in Germany.

Many people now wanted to join the Nazi Party. Wealthy people, government officials, and artists declared their support for Hitler. At the same time, however, many others were alarmed by Hitler. Important writers, scientists, and artists left the country.

By early 1933, Germany was a Nazi nation under the swastika flag. Under the absolute leadership of Hitler, people existed only to serve the state and obey the führer's words. Those who disagreed with him faced death.

As the dictator of Germany, Hitler now turned his attention to the anti-Semitic issues that had originally brought him into politics. On March 28, 1933, he called for all Germans to boycott Jewish businesses on April 1. It was the first act of the Holocaust.

CHAPTER 6

NAZI POWER SPREADS

On April 1, 1933, Nazi storm troopers stood in front of Jewish-owned shops. They held signs that read, "German people, defend yourselves. Don't buy from Jews." Anyone who dared to shop in Jewish stores was insulted, and some were attacked.

The boycott of Jewish stores lasted one day, but it marked the beginning of a widespread persecution of Jews by the Nazis. At the time, Jews made up fewer than one percent of the population of Germany. Many were patriotic Germans who had served in World War I. Yet, to Hitler and the Nazis, Jews were a menace to the nation and a threat to the Aryan race.

Hitler greeted crowds with his stiff-arm salute.

Six days after the boycott, Hitler introduced "The Law for the Restoration of the Civil Service." This law forced Jews out of civil service positions. On April 22, Jews were banned from positions in state-operated institutions, such as hospitals and universities. On April 25, Jewish children were forced to leave public schools. On September 29, Jews were banned from employment in literature, art, film, and theater. By October, Jews were forbidden to work as journalists, and all German newspapers were taken over by the Nazis.

Once in power, Nazis burned "un-German" books.

Book Burning in Berlin

As Hitler put his anti-Semitic policies in place, he and the Nazis also attacked the intellectual development of Germany. As a young man, Hitler liked to read and enjoyed history, German myth, and philosophy, but as a high-school dropout, he resented intellectuals, as well as most types of literature.

On May 10, 1933, under Hitler's orders, the Nazis burned thousands of books in a huge bonfire in front of the Berlin Opera House. Some of the books were classics of literature and philosophy written by Jews. Other books were destroyed because they advocated so-called un-German ideas.

The Nazis recruited students to throw books into the bonfire. Goebbels, who had a degree in literature, joined the group. He declared, "The era of extreme Jewish intellectualism is now at an end. . . . The future German man will not just be a man of books, but a man of character . . . you do well in this midnight hour to commit to the flames the evil spirit of the past."

The book burning was Hitler's first step as he moved to take control of the nation's education system. Soon, all teachers from elementary school to university level were either Nazi supporters or had been intimidated into silence. Young people learned Nazi propaganda in classrooms from teachers whose only qualification was party membership.

At first, young Nazi thugs were arrested by regular police.

The unforeseen result of the new educational program was the creation of a generation of young people who were ignorant in math and science. A commander in the German army complained that officer recruits displayed "a simply inconceivable lack of elementary knowledge."

Hitler was not concerned. He wanted an educational system that taught German children one main lesson—absolute obedience to the state. Young people learned that the life of the individual did not matter; only the survival of the German Reich was important.

"My program for educating youth is hard," Hitler said. "I want a brutal, domineering, fearless, cruel youth. . . . There must be nothing weak and gentle about it. . . . That is how I will eradicate thousands of years of human domestication [civilization]."

Problems in the Nazi Party

In the spring of 1934, the persecution of Jews continued with a campaign for "Jew free" villages. Nazi SA troops often struck villages in the middle of the night and took Jews from their homes. They beat and sometimes killed these victims.

Ernst Röhm tried to lead a revolt against Hitler.

As the power of the SA grew, the force became a menace not only to Jews but also to other Germans, including Hitler himself. The leader of the SA, Ernst Röhm, had supported Hitler since the Nazi Party began. As Röhm's force grew larger, German military leaders became concerned that the SA had become more powerful than the nation's army.

In February 1934, Hitler met with Röhm and told him that the SA would no longer be a military force. The storm troopers would be used only to maintain order at political functions. Röhm outwardly agreed with Hitler, but in private, he called Hitler a traitor and threatened to lead a revolt against him.

Word of Röhm's threats reached several Nazis who were loyal to Hitler, including Göring and two leaders of the SS, Heinrich Himmler and Reinhard Heydrich. These three men saw an opportunity to topple Röhm and gain greater power for themselves. For much of the winter and spring of 1934, they tried to persuade Hitler to take action against Röhm.

In late June 1934, Hitler gave orders to arrest Röhm and several hundred SA leaders. Also arrested were personal enemies of Göring, Himmler, and Heydrich. In an event that came to be called "The Night of the Long Knives," Röhm, his closest assistants, and nearly 1,000 other Germans were executed by SS firing squads on June 30, 1934.

Hitler knew that he needed a better way to control dissent. In order to make certain that his followers were loyal and that anti-Semitic laws and educational policies were obeyed, Hitler transformed the Gestapo that had been formed a year earlier. Hitler decided that the Gestapo would become a plainclothes force. It would depend on paid informers and keep secret files on the private lives of Germans from all backgrounds, including even the officials closest to Hitler himself.

In April 1934 Göring turned the Gestapo over to Himmler and Heydrich. Together, they made the Gestapo one of the most feared of all Nazi organizations, with spies who seemed to be everywhere. Germans were terrified to utter even the mildest criticism of Hitler for fear of arrest.

On February 10, 1936, the Gestapo law went into effect. It stated that "Neither the instructions nor the affairs of the Gestapo will be open to review by the administrative courts." This law placed the Gestapo beyond the control of the courts. As Hitler put it, "All means, even if they are not in conformity with existing laws and precedents, are legal if they subserve the will of the Führer."

The Unchallenged Führer

During the first half of the 1930s, Hitler was hampered by two obstacles in his attempts to assume complete control of Germany: the president and the military. In 1934, Hindenburg was 87 years old and in poor health. Hitler wanted to succeed Hindenburg, but did not want to become merely the president. Instead, he wanted to be declared the führer, or supreme leader, of Germany.

On August 2, 1934, Hindenburg died. Immediately, the Nazi-controlled Reichstag announced the passage of a law that combined the office of president with that of chancellor and transferred all power to the führer, Adolf Hitler. The law violated the German constitution's rule of presidential succession. It also violated the Enabling Act of 1933, which prohibited any changes in the office of president. Those violations did not matter. No political force was powerful enough to oppose the Nazi regime.

In order to exert control over the military, Hitler forced the German Officer Corps and every soldier in the army to swear allegiance not just to Germany but to him personally. Two weeks later, Hitler, the man Hindenburg had called the "Austrian Corporal" behind his back, addressed a rally of more than 150,000 supporters. He proclaimed, "The German form of life is definitely determined for the next thousand years!"

Hitler also used his increased power to continue attacks on Jews. In September 1935, Nazis held a huge meeting at Nuremberg, where several new laws were passed. One stated that only a person of "German or related blood" could be a German citizen. Another law, called the "Law for Protection of German Blood and German Honor" made it illegal for Jews and other Germans to marry. The Nuremberg laws stripped Jews of all their civil rights. They also segregated Jews from the other members of German society.

Heinrich Himmler was one of Hitler's closest associates.

The First Concentration Camps

Despite the outward acceptance of Nazism by most Germans, Hitler's policies caused a great deal of outrage and dissent. In addition to Jews, Communists, Christian religious leaders, and anyone who spoke out against the Nazis were arrested. As early as 1933, the numbers of people arrested had become too large for jails to hold. To fix this problem, Himmler established what came to be called a concentration camp at Dachau, 12 miles from Munich, to house all opponents of the Reich. Himmler appointed Theodor Eicke, a fanatical Nazi, to run the camp.

Eicke set strict rules that included hanging if a prisoner refused to obey the orders of the SS guards. Prisoners were beaten for the slightest offense or placed in solitary confinement cells so small they had to stand up. Prisoners had their heads shaved and had to wear blue-striped clothes. They were forced to work 12 hours a day at hard labor while the SS guards called them "pigs" and "filth." The ashes of those who died or were executed were put in containers and left on the doorsteps of their families. To explain the deaths, officials said the prisoners had been "shot while trying to escape."

Himmler was so impressed with Eicke's management of Dachau that he named him the first Inspector of Concentration Camps in July 1934. Within a year, there were 50 concentration camps built in Germany, all of which used Dachau as a model. The camps included Buchenwald in central Germany, Sachsenhausen near Berlin, and Ravensbruck, the camp for women. As word of the concentration camps spread across Germany, it was a clear warning about what could happen to anyone who disagreed with the Nazis.

Expansion Beyond German Borders

Besides anti-Semitism, the other main component of the Nazi philosophy was lebensraum, land for Germans. Hitler began to implement that phase of his policy in March 1935, when he announced to his cabinet that Germany would defy the Treaty of Versailles and rebuild its military. He planned to draft young men to build a new army with 36 divisions—a total of more than 500,000 soldiers. Several weeks later, Hitler approved a secret plan that put Germany's industries to work to build ships, tanks, planes, and weapons.

Word of these steps was not well received by the German general staff, who were lifelong military officers from military families that traced back for centuries. The idea that a mere corporal—and a non-German—could command them was insulting. Hitler overcame the resistance in the same way he overcame most resistance—with the Gestapo. As the Germany military rearmed, powerful German generals disappeared, including Schleicher who had been murdered during the Night of the Long Knives in 1934. Press notices said that certain generals had retired "for reasons of health." Commanders who agreed to accept Hitler's direction took over the military high command. These included Göring, who became commander of the newly formed German air force.

On March 7, 1936, three battalions of the German army crossed the Rhine River and took control of an industrial region known as the Rhineland, which Germany had surrendered to the Allies after World War I. The territory bordered France, but the much larger French army never threatened the 30,000 German troops that entered the area. Although the Treaty of Versailles stated that both France and England controlled the Rhineland, both countries had serious economic problems and neither took military action.

Hitler had gambled and won, but his bold actions had alarmed people in many nations, including Germany. To reassure those who were concerned about the possibility of another world war, Hitler gave a speech in which he said that Germany "shall strive for an understanding between European peoples, especially... with our Western neighbor nations.... We have no territorial demands to make in Europe.... Germany will never break the peace."

This made Germans feel better as they went to the polls to vote on the occupation of the Rhineland. Almost all eligible German voters took part in the referendum, and the occupation was approved by 98.8 percent.

Commander of the Armed Forces

In 1937, Hitler continued to give other nations a false sense of the Nazis' intent. On November 5, 1937, the führer signed a treaty with Poland that promised Germany would not invade the country. That same afternoon, Hitler held a secret meeting with his cabinet and top commanders. As he began the meeting, he stated that Germans, as a "master race," were entitled to "greater living space than in the case of other peoples."

Hitler then laid out his lebensraum plans to take land from other nations for the benefit of the German people. His ultimate goal lay across Poland in the vast Soviet Union. Before he invaded that region, he planned to occupy Austria and Czechoslovakia in order to protect Germany from the southeast. While all this was done, said Hitler, Germany had to make certain that Great Britain and France did not take action against the moves. In other words, he planned to lie to the British and French as he had done the Poles.

By February 1938, Hitler had abolished the War Ministry and replaced it with the High Command of the Armed Forces—and named himself the leader. Just over five years after he became chancellor, Hitler had total political and military control over Germany.

On March 12, 1938, German tanks crossed the German-Austrian border and met no resistance. In some places, in fact, the German invaders were hailed as heroes. More than 7 million ethnic Germans in Austria wanted to live under the führer's rule.

When Hitler learned of the welcome the German troops had received, he led a unit of soldiers to his birthplace at Branau am Inn and visited the graves of his family. He continued on to Linz, where he said, "Providence once called me forth from this town to be the leader of the Reich, it must in doing so . . . restore my dear homeland to the German Reich."

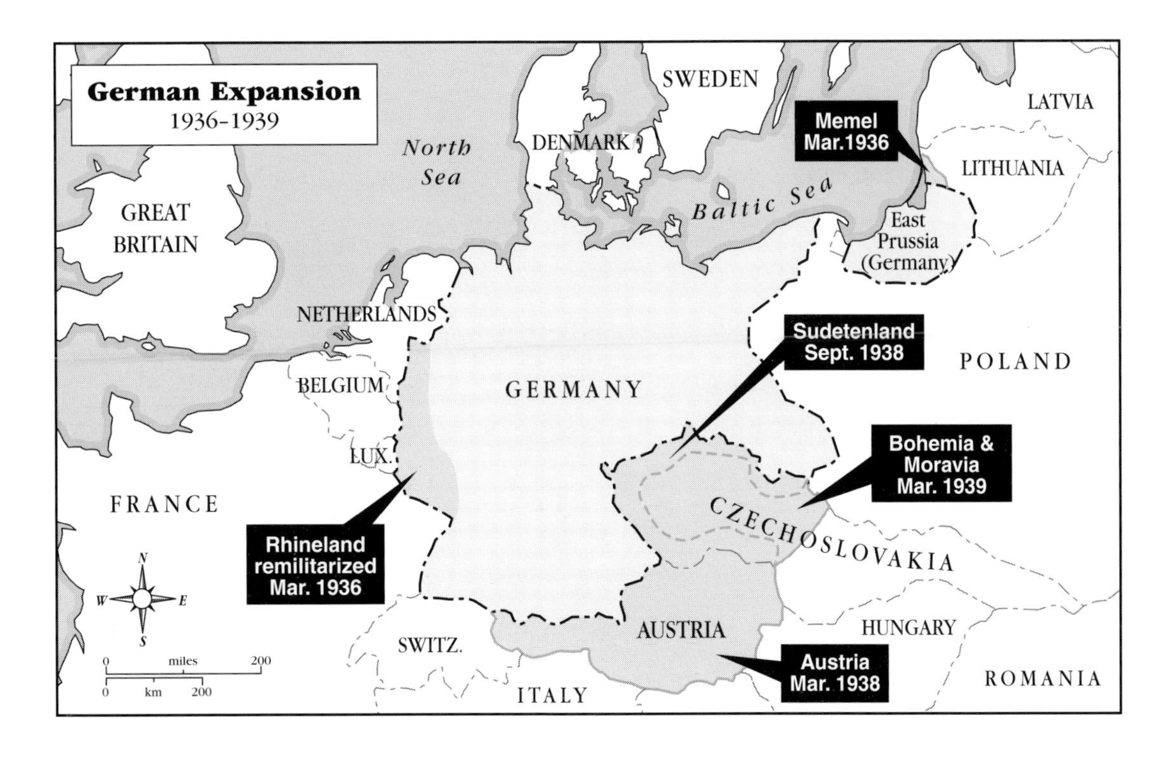

From Linz, Hitler went to Vienna, the city in which he had lived as a homeless drifter almost 30 years earlier. Cheering crowds lined the streets as he made his way to the Hotel Imperial.

The sudden arrival of Nazis in Austria encouraged a large number of Austrians to join the Nazi Party. This resulted in an outbreak of anti-Semitism more violent than any that had yet occurred in Germany. Much of the violence took place in Vienna, which had a population of 180,000 Jews. Nazis attacked and arrested Jews in the street. SS troops forced Jewish men and women to clean public toilets with sacred Hebrew prayer shawls. Thousands of Jews were jailed for no reason other than that they were Jewish, and police stood by while Nazis looted Jewish homes and businesses.

Hitler's bold move into Austria and his increasingly grand plans for conquest now alarmed powerful Germans who had once supported him. In addition, a small number of these influential Germans had witnessed Hitler's rages and had become concerned that he might not be entirely sane. A German doctor wrote in his journal that Hitler "was a border case between genius and insanity and . . . in . . . the near future. . . . Hitler's mind could swing toward the latter."

In the summer of 1938, General Ludwig Beck and several other top German generals met in secret to voice their concerns about Hitler's next goal, the western region of Czechoslovakia known as the Sudetenland. The group developed a plan to overthrow Hitler and put him on trial for treason. To accomplish such a revolutionary task, they felt that they needed the support of Great Britain and France. The generals sent agents to Great Britain to inform British leaders of the plot.

Once again, Hitler deceived Great Britain and France. He promised the British and French that all he wanted was the Sudetenland. The British chose to believe Hitler rather than agents from the German army, and the plot against him never took root.

Once Great Britain and France had accepted his goal, Hitler sought the approval of other European countries. In a secret meeting in early September 1938, Hitler agreed to give the leaders of Hungary and Poland the right to take other sections of Czechoslovakia if they accepted German control of the Sudetenland. Several weeks later, on September 29, Hitler met in Munich with representatives of Great Britain and France. Benito Mussolini, the dictator of Italy, also attended the meeting. Mussolini and Hitler had already reached an agreement that would permit Germany to take all of Czechoslovakia without Italy's interference. Hitler was able to convince British and French leaders that he intended only to take the Sudetenland.

On October 1, 1938, the German army crossed into Sudetenland without resistance. For the third time in two years, Hitler had taken a large area of land without firing a shot. His success increased his contempt for his former enemies in World War I. "Our enemies are little worms," he said. "I saw them at Munich."

The Path to World War II

The relative ease with which Hitler had taken control of large amounts of territory led him to believe that other nations of Europe were powerless to oppose him. He began to think that the Third Reich could conquer the world.

Hitler also decided that he could implement stronger anti-Semitic measures without objection from European leaders. Several weeks after Germany took the Sudetenland, he ordered the SS to arrest about 17,000 Polish Jews who lived in Germany. Hitler ordered the families back to Poland. They were loaded onto trains, taken to the Polish border, and unloaded. Poland refused to admit them because they were considered German citizens. As winter set in, thousands of men, women, and children were stranded at the Polish border with only the clothes on their back.

One family of deported Jews was named Grynszpan. Their teenage son, Herschel, lived in Paris at the time of the deportation. When he learned about the fate of his family, Grynszpan decided to take revenge on the Nazis. On November 7, he forced his way into the office of a Nazi diplomat in Paris and shot him. The Nazi died on the evening of November 9. His death began the night known as *Kristallnacht*—the Night of the Broken Glass.

Hitler and the Nazis were widely condemned by other nations for the terror of *Kristallnacht*. Before that event, groups of Hitler supporters had arisen in various countries, including the United States. After *Kristallnacht*, much of the world began to see Hitler and the Nazis as criminals. By then, however, it was too late to stop them, because over the last three years, Germany had rearmed and rebuilt its military into the most powerful armed force in Europe, even though German forces were supposed to be limited by the Treaty of Versailles.

On March 15, 1939, the president of Czechoslovakia surrendered his country to Hitler, who had threatened to destroy half of Prague with the German air force within two hours. The Czech president wrote that he had "confidently placed the fate of

The damage from Kristallnacht *in the streets and in synagogues shocked the world.*

Hitler spoke to the Reichstag to declare war on Poland.

the Czech people and country in the hands of the Führer of the German Reich."

The conquest of Czechoslovakia broke the agreement Hitler had made six months earlier with Great Britain and France. It now became apparent to them that Hitler's next target would be Poland. The British and French warned Hitler that an attack on Poland would lead them to declare war on Germany.

By this point, Hitler had no fear of either Great Britain or France. His only concern was whether the Soviet Union, on Poland's eastern border, would use a German attack as an excuse to launch an attack of its own on Germany. To avoid a confrontation with the Soviet Union, Hitler signed a pact with Soviet leader Joseph Stalin on August 23. The agreement offered the Soviets the right to take eastern Poland if they allowed Germany to attack.

Hitler still needed an excuse to invade a peaceful country. To justify his actions, he secretly ordered false attacks on German troops who were massed at the Polish border. On August 31, SS troops in Polish army uniforms staged border attacks on German troops. The Germans took over a radio station and announced in Polish, "People of Poland, the time has come for war between Poland and Germany!"

Hitler now had his excuse to launch the invasion. He was confident that Great Britain and France would not take any action. Hitler spoke to his generals before he gave the final order to attack: "Close your eyes to pity! Act brutally.... The stronger man is right! Be harsh and remorseless!"

On Friday morning, September 1, 1939, German troops crossed into Poland and smashed all resistance in a blitzkrieg—"lightning war." Polish troops fought bravely, but they were outnumbered and their equipment was out of date. Some Polish units fought on horseback against German tanks and bombers.

On September 3, Great Britain and France declared war on Germany. World War II had begun.

Chapter 7

War and the Holocaust

It took German forces less than one month to reach Warsaw, the capital of Poland. On September 27, Poland surrendered. This placed Poland's 2 million Jews—the largest Jewish population in Europe—under Nazi control. Germany partitioned the nation and gave a large part of eastern Poland to the Soviet Union.

After his lightning victory over Poland, Hitler turned his army to the West to dispense with the Allied nations. In April 1940, Hitler's forces swept through Norway and Denmark. In May and June, the Netherlands, Belgium, France, and Luxembourg fell to German

German forces overwhelmed Polish resistance as they raced through the countryside.

troops. On June 22, a triumphant Hitler forced France to sign an armistice at Compiègne.

Once France had fallen, Hitler ordered Göring's air force to bomb Great Britain. Waves of German bombers attacked London and other large British cities throughout 1941 and 1942.

For the first two years of the war, Hitler's forces appeared to be unstoppable. Many nations feared that the Nazis would eventually dominate the world. They did not know that in many ways, Hitler's lack of leadership qualities had already begun to weaken him. One flaw was his inability to make a decision. For example, on August 26, a week before the Polish invasion, Hitler almost called the attack off because he suddenly feared the British would honor their agreement to help Poland.

An aide described how strangely Hitler behaved when he was told that it was likely the British would defend Poland: "The Führer suddenly got up, and becoming very nervous, walked up and down. . . . suddenly he stopped in the middle of the room and stood there staring. His voice was blurred, and his behavior that of a completely abnormal person. He spoke in staccato phrases: 'If there should be war, then I shall build U-boats, [submarines] build U-boats, U-boats, U-boats, U-boats' . . . then he pulled himself together, raised his voice as though addressing a large audience and shrieked: 'I shall build airplanes, build airplanes, airplanes, airplanes, and I shall annihilate my enemies!'"

Once Hitler did make a decision, his other flaws came to the surface. He refused to admit it when he had made an error or consider that he should alter his plan. Just as he had done when he was a young man, Hitler flew into rages when he was contradicted. Germans in the Nazi high command frequently witnessed tantrums in which the führer's face turned beet red. He then screamed, cursed, punched furniture, and crashed against the wall with his arms stretched out as if he were on a cross. Yet even if the Nazis closest to him had doubts about his abilities, Hitler's power was absolute.

The Holocaust

As the Nazis conquered millions of square miles in Europe, they also began the mass extermination of Jews and other groups that is known as the Holocaust. As the Germans moved across Poland, they terrorized the Jews. They cut off the beards of Jewish men. They attacked Jews on the streets. They forced Jews to wear a yellow Star of David—a Jewish religious symbol—on their clothing so they could be identified.

Reinhard Heydrich was one of Hitler's most feared and hated officials.

By December 1939, more than 120,000 Polish Jews were dead. At that time, Reinhard Heydrich, Himmler's top aide, began to develop "planned total measures" to deal with Jews. Hitler called Heydrich "the man with the iron heart," and he relied on Heydrich to interpret his orders in regard to Jews. One of the Nazis' most vicious anti-Semites, Heydrich was eager to find an efficient way to exterminate the millions of Jews who lived in Europe. His first act was to place all Jews into enclosed city areas called ghettos, where they would be held until the Nazis developed an efficient method of mass killing.

In 1940, ghettos were established in the Polish cities of Lodz, Kraków, and Warsaw. Those Jews who were crowded into the ghettos faced horrible conditions. About one-third of Warsaw's population was pushed into the ghetto, whose size was only 2 percent of the city's area. Fifteen people lived in a space big enough

German troops in Poland forced Jews into ghettos.

for four. The Germans allowed each person enough food to equal 800 calories a day, less than half the 2,000 calories most people needed.

In crowded conditions and near starvation, Jews—especially children and the elderly—came down with disease. Yet the Germans refused to allow any medicine into the ghetto. In 1940, more than 56,000 people died in the Warsaw ghetto alone.

A Jewish child who died was buried in the ghetto cemetery by adults.

In January 1940, the Nazis chose the village of Óswiecim, Poland, as the site for a new concentration camp. By the summer of 1941, the camp, called Auschwitz, had begun to receive trains that carried Jews, Poles, Roma, and other victims of Nazi conquest.

Outside the camps, it was the job of the SS to carry out Hitler's plan. Special units called *Einsatzgruppen* followed the German army into occupied areas. Their sole mission was to carry out mass killings of Jews in areas that fell under Nazi rule. The worst of these massacres occurred at Babi Yar, a village outside of Kiev, Ukraine. On September 29–30, 1941, the *Einsatzgruppen* herded Jews to the fields outside the village, shot them, and buried them in mass graves. Almost 34,000 Jews were murdered at Babi Yar.

Early in 1942, Nazi leaders met outside of Berlin to coordinate the annihilation of the Jews. Hitler was not present, but his wishes were understood by everyone there. At the time the meeting took place, the six large concentration camps were undergoing a change. They soon became death camps. All of the camps were located near large cities in Poland. Railroad lines connected the camps to large population centers so that Jews could easily be brought there. At the meeting of Nazi leaders, Adolf Eichmann, a lieutenant colonel in charge of the SS Jewish Office, received an assignment to transport Jews from all parts of Europe to the Nazi death camps.

The largest death camp was Auschwitz. Others were located at Chelmno, Treblinka, Sobibor, Majdanek, and Belzec. Chelmno was completed first. More than 300,000 Jews died there. Treblinka, just east of Warsaw, opened in July 1942. About 900,000 Jews met their deaths in this camp. Only Auschwitz killed more Jews—more than one million were murdered there.

Trains brought Jews to Auschwitz from all over Europe. SS officers decided who would die first and who might live longer so they could work in the labor camp. The officers usually sent very young children, older people, and those who looked sick immediately to their deaths. Children were separated from their parents, and men were separated from women.

More than 12,000 people a day were killed at the Auschwitz death camp.

Those chosen to die were taken to large rooms, often marked "showers" or "baths." After the victims removed their clothing, a poison gas called Zyklon B was pumped in through vents. This gas killed everyone in the room within 15 to 20 minutes. The bodies were then burned in furnaces. At its height of operation, about 12,000 people were murdered at Auschwitz each day. Many of the Jews and other people who were not killed upon arrival to the camps later were shot to death, died of starvation, or were worked to death.

Defeat and Death

By the middle of 1941, the Nazi army had conquered territory that stretched from North Africa across Europe to the border of the Soviet Union. In late June, Hitler ordered his army to attack the Soviet Union, which violated the pact he had signed with Stalin. Up to that time, Hitler had avoided an invasion of the Soviet Union because he did not want to fight a two-front war against the Allied powers. With most of Western Europe under Nazi control, however, the army could focus on the lebensraum in the Soviet Union.

At first, the Nazis were successful with a blitzkrieg across the open lands of the western Soviet Union. As military units raced eastward, SS killers followed and carried out some of the worst mass executions of civilians in history. By late 1941, the Germans had reached the outskirts of Moscow, the Soviet capital.

At that point, the Germans' progress slowed for the first time in six months. Winter—a brutally cold season in Russia—set in, and the army's equipment, such as tanks, planes, and other mechanized vehicles, became almost useless. Then, on December 6, 1941, the Soviet army launched its first major counterattack against the Nazis.

The next day, December 7, 1941, thousands of miles away at Pearl Harbor, Hawaii, the Japanese launched a surprise attack on the United States. Throughout the 1930s, Japan had tried to expand its borders in an effort to become the dominant power in Asia. Japan had formed an alliance with Hitler's Germany and Mussolini's Italy, which were known together as the Axis powers. On December 8, the United States declared war on Japan. Although the United States had not entered the war in Europe, the American government had loaned ships and other military equipment to Great Britain. Hitler, who despised the American system of democracy, felt that the United States was too weak to become involved in a two-front war in both the Pacific and Europe. Germany declared war on the United States on December 11.

As 1942 began, the Axis powers had the upper hand in the war. That changed by the fall of 1942, when the Germans were locked in a bloody fight against the Soviets that threatened to destroy the German army. American forces had won a victory in the Pacific and had landed in North Africa. The Soviet army in southern Europe had defeated the Italians, who surrendered in 1943.

It was during these years that Hitler's personal flaws became most apparent. His inability to recognize that his army could not defeat the Soviets made the war in

Allied forces landed in Normandy on June 6, 1944.

the East a disaster for Germany. A furious Hitler insisted that his army should fight to the last man, but by late 1943, the German army in the East was in retreat.

At the same time, Allied forces had driven the Germans out of North Africa and invaded Italy, while Allied bombers attacked German industrial cities. By 1944, in Great Britain, the Allies had begun to make preparations for an invasion of German-controlled France at Normandy.

Hitler insisted that the Allies would invade at Calais, a point closer to Great Britain, many miles northwest of Normandy. He ordered his most powerful tank units stationed there. When the Allies invaded at Normandy on D-Day, June 6, 1944, there were no German tanks to defend the area.

As the Nazis faced military setbacks, Hitler's health deteriorated. He was known to be a hypochondriac who complained constantly of aches and pains. By mid-1942, however, he had developed noticeable tremors in his hands and head. His mental processes were slow and his rages more volcanic than ever. He also battled insomnia, an inability to sleep, which further affected his thought processes.

Many of the symptoms Hitler exhibited were signs of Parkinson's disease, a degenerative nerve disorder. Doctors gave Hitler drug injections to help him sleep and others to keep him alert, but these treatments worsened his already fragile condition. There is no definite proof that Hitler had a nerve disease, but problems with his thought processes, such as his inability to make quick decisions and his refusal to change his mind, played a major role in the Nazis' reversal of fortune. By July 1944, German forces were in retreat across both Western and Eastern Europe.

On July 20, a group of German civilians and generals, who realized that Germany had already lost the war, tried to assassinate Hitler. The attempt failed, but it made Hitler's mental condition even more unstable. He became convinced that he was invincible and that voices spoke to him as he claimed they had during his close calls in World War I. In a rage, he ordered the SS to kill every family member, including the children, of all those who participated in the plot against him—which led to the execution of more than 5,000 people. He ordered the top six military officers involved in the plot hung on meat hooks and slowly strangled. Hitler had the gruesome spectacle filmed. He then ordered the film to be shown to all army recruits as a warning that no one should disobey the führer.

Russian troops rolled through eastern Germany in 1944.

Four days after the assassination attempt, Soviet forces raced across Poland and liberated the Nazi death camp at Majdanek. Although the camp had not eliminated Jews and other groups of people on a huge scale like Auschwitz, the world finally saw evidence of the Nazis' plans to wipe out their enemies.

By late 1944, Hitler's days were numbered. Around Christmas, the

German army made one last effort to counterattack Allied forces in Belgium, but it was overwhelmed. German cities lay in ruins as the Allies closed in from the West and the Soviets approached from the East.

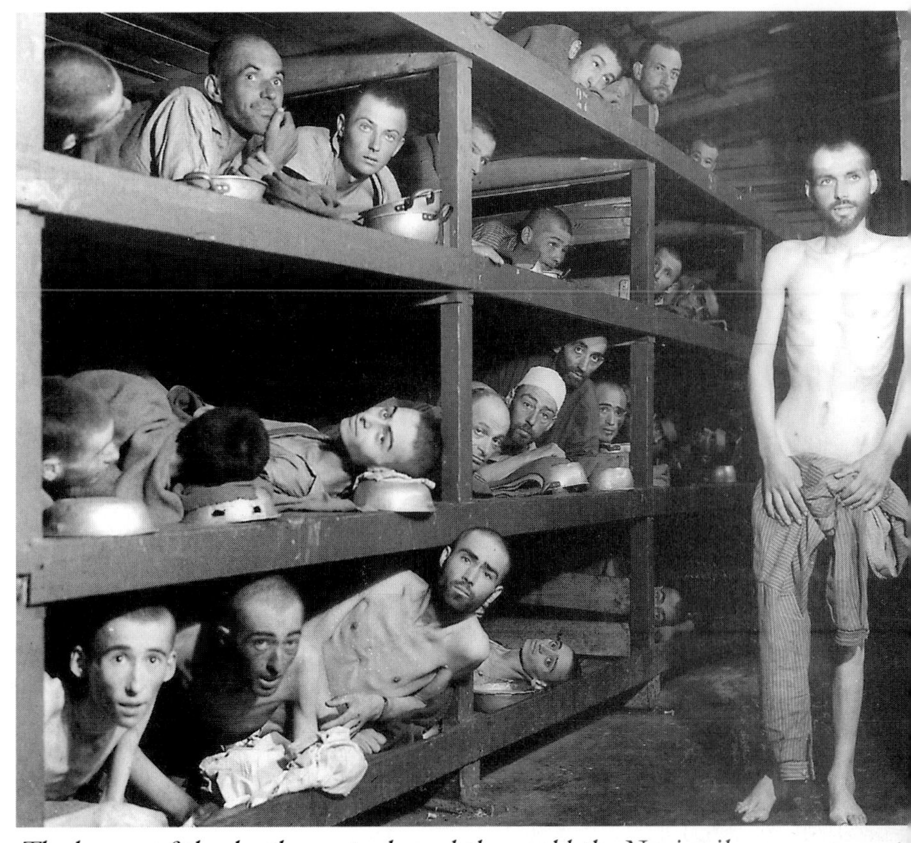

The horror of the death camps showed the world the Nazi evil.

In April 1945, Hitler moved into the *Führerbunker*, an underground complex of about 30 rooms on two separate floors. There he met with his generals hourly, and followed the progress of the Soviet army toward Berlin. Hitler ordered that Berlin be defended at all costs. The army to which he issued orders, however, was broken and prepared to surrender to the Allies.

On April 22, Hitler went into a hysterical tirade. As usual, he blamed the Jews and Communists, but this time, he knew that the end had come. The Third Reich had failed. His closest aides tried to convince Hitler to escape to the mountains, but he refused. Most of Hitler's staff fled the bunker. Only a few people remained, including Goebbels, some SS and military aides, two of Hitler's secretaries, and Eva Braun.

Around noon on April 30, Hitler learned that the Soviets were about a block away. He told his chauffeur to bring 200 liters of gasoline to the garden above the bunker. Hitler and Braun returned to their private quarters. Moments later, a gunshot rang out. Goebbels went into Hitler's room and found Hitler on the sofa, dead from a gunshot wound to his right temple. Braun, who had taken poison, was also dead. The bodies were carried up to the garden. Aides covered them with gasoline and set fire to them. Goebbels gave a final Nazi salute. Then the charred remains were buried in a huge hole made by an artillery shell explosion.

Epilogue

The German army surrendered one week after Hitler's suicide, on May 7, 1945. Many of Hitler's closest Nazi associates, including Goebbels, Himmler, and Göring, committed suicide. Heydrich was assassinated by Czech fighters. Other Nazis were tried for war crimes and some were executed. Eichmann escaped to South America, but he was arrested in 1960 and brought to the Jewish state of Israel, where he was put on trial and executed.

Hitler had predicted that the Third Reich would last 1,000 years. In fact, it barely lasted 12 years. That a man who had been a high school dropout and a drifter could convince others to help him eliminate entire groups of people and to try to rule the world is almost unbelievable.

Even Hitler knew that his absolute power was built on falsehoods. In *Mein Kampf* he wrote:

Goebbels (left) and Goring(right) committed suicide.

> *The size of the lie is a definite factor in causing it to be believed, for the vast masses of the nation are in the depths of their hearts more easily deceived than they are consciously and intentionally bad. The primitive simplicity of their minds renders them a more easy prey to a big lie than a small one, for they themselves often tell little lies but would be ashamed to tell a big one.*

Chronology

1889	**April 20:** Hitler is born.
1907	**October:** Hitler fails art exam.
	December 21: Hitler's mother dies.
1914–1918	World War I.
1919	Hitler joins German Workers' Party.
1921	**July:** Hitler named leader of Nazi Party.
1923	**November:** Beer Hall Putsch fails.
1929	**October:** Great Depression begins.
1932–1933	Great famine in Sovet Union.
1933	**January 20:** Hitler named chancellor of Germany.
	March 23: Hitler becomes dictator of Germany.
	May 10: Burning of books.
1934	**June 30:** Night of the Long Knives.
1936	**March 7:** Nazis march into Rhineland.
1938	**November 9:** Night of Broken Glass.
1939	**March 12:** Nazis take Austria.
	March 15: Nazis take Czechoslovakia.
	August 23: Nazi-Soviet nonaggression pact.
	September 1: Nazis invade Poland; World War II begins.

1940	**May 10:** Nazis invade France, Belgium, Luxembourg, and the Netherlands.
	August 15: Air battles and daylight raids over Britain.
1941	**June 22:** Germany invades Soviet Union.
	September 29: Nazis murder 33,771 Jews at Kiev.
	December 6: Soviet Army launches a major counteroffensive around Moscow.
	December 7: Japanese bomb Pearl Harbor.
	December 8: United States and Britain declare war on Japan.
1942	**June:** Mass murder of Jews by gassing begins at Auschwitz.
1943	**February 2:** Germans surrender at Stalingrad in the first big defeat of Hitler's army.
1944	**June 6:** Allies land at Normandy.
	July 20: German assassination attempt on Hitler fails.
	July 24: Soviet troops liberate first concentration camp at Majdanek.
1945	**January 26:** Soviet troops liberate Auschwitz.
	April 21: Soviets reach Berlin.
	April 30: Hitler commits suicide.

Glossary

Allies The nations that fought against Germany, Italy, and Japan in World War II: Great Britain, France, the Soviet Union, and the United States

anti-Semitism Extreme prejudice against Jews

artillery Large weapons used by fighting forces, usually cannons and mortars

Auschwitz Largest concentration camp and death camp

boycott To refuse to do business or associate with a certain individual or group

concentration camp A prison and labor camp built to hold people the Nazis considered dangerous; prisoners usually died there from hard labor, disease, or starvation

conspiracy A secret plot or plan to commit a wrongful or unlawful act

death camp A camp built by Nazis specifically to murder Jews and other groups of people

division Military group of between 6,000 to 8,000 soldiers

Einsatzgruppen Special SS unit assigned to kill Jews

"Final Solution" Term used by Nazis to refer to their plan to completely exterminate the Jewish people

führer Supreme leader

gas chamber Airtight room sealed off to kill people through the use of poison gas

genocide The systematic attempt to wipe out an entire people

Gestapo Secret police set up to eliminate opposition to Hitler and the Nazi party

ghetto A section of a city where a particular group of people is forced to live

Holocaust The systematic, planned extermination of European Jews and other groups by the Nazis during World War II

propaganda Information spread to influence or mislead people

regiment A military unit smaller than a brigade (300 to 1,000 soldiers) and a division

scapegoat A person who is blamed for another's problems, mistakes, or crimes

SS Members of Hitler's elite force whose responsibility was to carry out the "Final Solution" and run the concentration and death camps

storm trooper Member of an elite Nazi organization responsible for regular attacks on Jews and anyone opposed to the Nazis

synagogue Jewish house of prayer and religious study

Zyklon B A poison gas the Nazis used to kill victims in gas chambers

Source Notes

Introduction

Page 5: "rise in bloody vengeance . . . " *The Triumph of Hitler* History Place web site http://www.historyplace.com/worldwar2/triumph/tr-knacht.htm

Chapter 1

Page 14: "In our country " *The Heritage of Bismarck* web site http://mars.acnet.wnec.edu/~grempel/courses/germany/lectures/12bismarck.html

Page 16: "exceedingly violent and high strung." *The Rise of Hitler* The History Place web site http://www.historyplace.com/worldwar2/riseofhitler/art.htm

Page 17: "unsatisfactory" Ibid.

Chapter 2

Page 23: "anti-Christ . . . worse than devils." *Classical and Christian Anti-Semitism* web site http://www.remember.org/guide/History.root.classical.html

Page 24: "when Hitler became excited . . . " *The Rise of Hitler* The History Place web site http://www.historyplace.com/worldwar2/riseofhitler/art.htm

Page 27: "We pushed [the bodies] into the sides . . . " Photos of the Great War web site http://www.ku.edu/~kansite/ww_one/photos/greatwar.htm

Page 28: " . . . the greatest and most unforgettable time . . . " *The Rise of Hitler* The History Place web site http://www.historyplace.com/worldwar2/riseofhitler/art.htm

Chapter 3

Page 29 "We crawl on our stomachs . . . " *Extremes in No Man's Land* web site http://www.geocities.com/~worldwar1/remarque-eng.html

Page 30: "I was eating my dinner . . . " Ibid.

Chapter 4

Page 38: "One of the participants . . . " *The Rise of Hitler* The History Place web site http://www.historyplace.com/worldwar2/riseofhitler/

Page 39: "I spoke for thirty minutes . . . " Ibid.

Page 40: "It makes no difference . . . " *Adolf Hitler: Perverse Political Genius* web site

http://www.rjgeib.com/thoughts/hitler/hitler.html

Page 42: "Master race . . . eternally anti-Semitic." *The Swastika and the*

Nazis web site http://www.intelinet.org/swastika/swasti16.htm

Page 50: "Anyone who examines . . ." *What are "The Protocols of the Elders of Zion"?* web site http://www.holocaust-history.org/short-essays/protocols.shtml

Page 53: An instrument for the conduct . . ." *The Triumph of Hitler* History Place web site http://www.historyplace.com/worldwar2/triumph/

Chapter 5

Page 63: "It is almost like a dream . . ." *The Triumph of Hitler* History Place web site http://www.historyplace.com/worldwar2/triumph/

Page 63 "I prophesy to you this evil . . ." Ibid.

Page 66: "No enabling act can give you . . ." Ibid.

Page 66: "You are no longer needed!" Ibid.

Chapter 6

Page 70: "The era of extreme Jewish intellectualism . . ." *The Triumph of Hitler* History Place web site http://www.historyplace.com/worldwar2/triumph/

Page 72: "My program for educating youth is hard." *Adolf Hitler: Perverse Political Genius* web site http://www.rjgeib.com/thoughts/hitler/hitler.html

Page 79: "shall strive for an understanding . . ." *The Triumph of Hitler* History Place web site http://www.history-place.com/worldwar2/triumph/

Page 80: "Providence once called me forth . . ." Ibid.

Page 82: "was a border case . . ." *Adolf Hitler: Perverse Political Genius* web site http://www.rjgeib.com/thoughts/hitler/hitler.html

Page 83: "our enemies are little worms . . ." *The Triumph of Hitler* History Place web site http://www.historyplace.com/worldwar2/triumph/

Page 85: "confidently placed the fate . . ." Ibid.

Chapter 7

Page 90: "The Fuhrer suddenly got up . . ." *The Triumph of Hitler* History Place web site http://www.history-place.com/worldwar2/triumph/

Page 103: "The size of the lie . . ." *Adolf Hitler: Perverse Political Genius* web site http://www.rjgeib.com/thoughts/hitler/hitler.html

For Further Reading

Banyard, Peter. *The Rise of the Dictators 1919–1939*. Danbury, CT: Franklin Watts, 1986.

Bauer, Yehuda. *A History of the Holocaust*, rev. ed. Danbury, CT: Franklin Watts, 2002.

Lace, William W. *Hitler and the Nazis*. San Diego: Gale Group, 2000.

Marrin, Albert. *Hitler*. New York: Viking, 1987.

Rice, Earle. *The Fall of the Third Reich: Demise of the Nazi Dream*. San Diego: Gale Group, 2000.

Stone, Norman. *Hitler*. Boston: Little, Brown, 1980.

Tames, Richard L. *Adolf Hitler*. Chicago: Heinemann Library, 1998.

Tolland, John. *Adolf Hitler*. New York: Doubleday, 1976.

Wepman, Dennis. *Adolf Hitler: German Dictator*. New York: Chelsea House, 1991.

Williamson, David. *The Third Reich*. New York: Bookwright, 1989.

Websites

Electing Adolf Hitler
http://www.calvin.edu/cas/gpa/hess2.htm

Hitler as Dictator
http://mars.acnet.wnec.edu/~grempel/courses

The Rise of Adolf Hitler
http://www.historyplace.com/worldwar2/riseofhitler/born.htm

Washington Post: The Death of Hitler
http://www.washingtonpost.com/we-srv/style/longterm/books/chap1/deathofhitler.htm

INDEX

Academy of Arts in Munich, 25
Academy of Fine Arts in Vienna, 17
Allied Powers (WWI), 33–35, 41, 44, 78
Allies (WWII), 88, 98–99, 101
anti–war sentiment, 31, 33, 35
Article 48, 55, 58–61
Aryans, 23, 49, 51, 68
Austro-Hungarian Empire, 13, 26
Axis Powers, 97

Bavaria, 10, 15, 25, 28, 38, 44–46, 48, 51
Beck, General Ludwig, 82
Beer Hall Putsch, 45–48
blitzkrieg, 87, 96
Bloch, Eduard, 18
Branau am Inn, 10, 12, 80
Brasol, Boris, 50
Braun, Eva, 62, 102
Brüning, Heinrich, 53, 57, 59

Catholic Center Party, 55
Catholic Church, 12, 14
Central Powers, 34
Christian Socialists, 24
Communist Manifesto, 32
Communists, 32, 34–36, 38, 40–41, 60, 64–65, 76, 101
concentration camps,
  Auschwitz, 93–95, 100
  Buchenwald, 77
  Chelmo, 94
  Dachau, 76–77
  Majdanek, 94, 100
  Ravensbruck, 77
  Sachsenhausen, 77
  Sobibor, 94
  Treblinka, 94

D-Day, 99
Diaspora, 22
Drexler, Anton, 39

Ebert, Friedrich, 37
Eichmann, Adolf, 94, 103
Eicke, Theodor, 76–77
Einsatzgruppen, 93
Enabling Act, 65–66, 75

Ferdinand, Archduke Franz, 26
Ford, Henry, 50
führer, 4, 43, 45, 67, 74–75, 79–80, 86, 90, 100

German Officer Corps, 75
German Workers Party, 38–41
Gestapo, 64, 73–74, 78
Goebbels, Joseph, 4–5, 7, 54, 63, 65, 70, 102
Göring, Hermann, 43, 45, 47–48, 62, 64, 73–74, 78, 89
Great Depression, 54–55
gypsies, 10, 93

Hapsburgs, 13
Heydrich, Reinhard, 73–74, 91, 102
Himmler, Heinrich, 73–74, 76–77, 91, 102
Hitler Youth, 52
Hitler, Adolf,
  beliefs and ideology, 20–21, 24–25, 31–32, 34, 36, 38–39, 42, 49–51, 54, 72, 97
  decline, 90–91, 93–94, 96–103
  formation and empowerment of Nazis, 39–48, 51–55
  führer of Germany, 4–5, 74–89
  growing up, 10, 12–13, 15–21, 23–26
  in prison, 48–49, 51
  in World War I, 28–32, 34–36, 100
  rise to power, 10, 56–73
  temperament, 12, 16–18, 20–21, 24, 38, 60, 66, 82, 90, 97, 99
Hitler, Alois, 10–13, 15–16
Hitler, Alois Jr., 12
Hitler, Angela, 12, 18
Hitler, Edmund, 12–13, 18
Hitler, Paula, 12, 16, 18

Inspector of Concentration Camps, 77
Iron Cross, 1st class, 34

Jehovah's Witnesses, 10
Jews,
  anti-Semitism, 20, 22–25, 32, 38–39, 42, 50, 67, 70, 73, 77, 81, 84, 91
  death of, 7, 10, 72, 91–95
  persecution of, 5, 7, 57, 68–69, 72, 75–76, 81, 84, 91–92
  imprisoned, 7, 76–77, 93–95

Kaiser, 14, 36
Kristallnacht, 5, 7, 84

Kubizek, August,
16–17, 19–20

Lebensraum, 51, 77,
79, 96
Luther, Martin, 22–23

Marr, William, 23
Marx, Karl, 32
Marxism, 32, 36–37,
40, 49
Mein Kampf, 49–52,
103
Mussolini, Benito, 83,
97
My Political Awakening,
39

National Socialist
German Workers
Party, 41
Nazis,
creation, 41–43
decline, 96–103
in power, 63–82,
84–85, 88–94
propaganda, 50,
64–65, 71
rise to power, 4–5, 7,
44–48, 51–62

Neumann, Josef, 24
Nicholas II, Czar, 32
Nuremburg laws, 75

Ortsgruppen, 52

Parkinson's Disease, 99
pogroms, 23
poison gas, 27, 34
Pölzl, Klara, 11–12,
16–18
Princip, Gavrilo, 26
Protocols of the Elders
of Zion, 50
Prussia, 14–15

Rachovsky, Pytor, 50
Reich, 14–15, 41, 63,
71, 76, 80, 86
Reichstag, 14, 36,
54–57, 59–61, 64,
66, 74, 86
Röhm, Ernst, 72–73
Russian Revolution,
32–33, 37

SA (Sturmabteilung),
45–46, 52–53,
58–60, 63–65,
72–73

Schicklgruber, Maria, 11
Second Reich, 36, 63
Social Democrats, 64,
66
Socialists, 14, 36
Somme, First Battle of
the, 31
SS (Schutzstaffel), 53,
58–60, 63–65, 73,
76, 84, 87, 93–94,
96, 100, 102
Stalin, Joseph, 87, 96
Strasser, Gregor, 62
swastika, 42, 53, 67

The International Jew,
50
The Law for the
Restoration of the
Civil Services, 69
The Night of the Long
Knives, 73, 78
Third Reich, 63, 84,
102–103
Treaty of Versailles,
34–35, 39, 42–43,
77–78, 85

University of Munich,
37

untermenschen, 49

Von Bismarck, Otto,
14–15, 36, 63
von Hindenburg,
Oskar, 62
von Hindenburg, Paul,
53, 55, 57–58,
60–61, 64, 66,
74–75
von Ludendorff, Erich,
63
von Papen, Franz,
59–62
von Schleicher, Kurt,
58–62, 78

Wagner, Richard, 20
Wall Street, 54
War Ministry, 80
Wels, Otto, 66
Wilhelm, Kaiser, 26–28
World War I, 26–35, 100
World War II, 9,
87–89, 96–98

Ypres, Battle of, 29–30

Zyklon B, 95